Don Richardson has always been an enthusiastic blazer of trails on lofty mountains, in New Guinea swamps rife with headhunters or boldly critiquing the Qur'an. Here he attempts no less than to lead us through Scripture and missions experience to the gates of Eternity itself. Don remains a pleasant companion on the trail as well as guide—personable, sincere, a font of stories, often finding new angles from which to view topography. Not every reader will follow him at each point—his extended critique of Calvinism and St. Augustine will seem bracing to some. But that is because this is not just a recreational stroll for Richardson, but literally a matter of life and death with the worldwide mission Christ gave us, which has already transformed the world for the better, at stake. In modern times, Christian faith needs to seek understanding with particular courage and imagination. Agree or disagree, Don Richardson takes up the challenge with exemplary boldness and he gave me, personally, a great deal to think about.

DR. DAVID MARSHALL

Author of *Jesus and the Religions of Man*
Editor of *Faith Seeking Understanding: Essays in Memory of
Paul Brand and Ralph D. Winter*

HEAVEN WINS

DON RICHARDSON

HEAVEN WINS

HEAVEN, HELL AND THE HOPE OF EVERY PERSON

Regal

For more information and
special offers from Regal Books, email us at
subscribe@regalbooks.com

Published by Regal
From Gospel Light
Ventura, California, U.S.A.
www.regalbooks.com
Printed in the U.S.A.

ISBN-13: 970-0-8307-6747-2

Rights for publishing this book outside the U.S.A. or in non-English
languages are administered by Gospel Light Worldwide, an international
not-for-profit ministry. For additional information, please visit www.glww.org,
email info@glww.org, or write to Gospel Light Worldwide,
1957 Eastman Avenue, Ventura, CA 93003, U.S.A.

To order copies of this book and other Regal products in bulk quantities,
please contact us at 1-800-446-7735.

To my beloved wife, Carol, who for these past eight
years has encompassed me with her love,
inspired me with her devotion to God
and partnered with me in our service for Him

CONTENTS

FOREWORD

eaven Wins affirms that God is winning and will win the battle for human souls. Souls in heaven will outnumber the souls in hell. Richardson reasons that this victory is necessary as a motivation for all the innumerable races of the entire universe to choose faithfulness to God—a speculative conclusion, but still very compatible with the Bible.

This numerical victory leads to two other doctrines. First, Richardson provides a scriptural and effective case that those who die before willfully choosing evil, i.e. before the "age of accountability," are God's. Statistics on pre-birth, infant and young child deaths affirm that these are the majority of human souls. Second, from Scripture he argues that natural revelation has brought salvific/ saving knowledge to many—more in Old Testament times than in the New Testament. Most of chapter 10 deals with examples of New Testament and modern-era "Jobs" who are taught by natural revelation and come to God in faith as a result.

This leads into Richardson's conviction that "none other name . . . whereby we must be saved" (Acts 4:12, *KJV*) does not mean that accurately voicing a pronunciation or understanding of the words "Lord Jesus Christ" is essential for redemption. (This reviewer had no understanding of *Christos* when he accepted forgiveness.). Rather, the concept of "name" deals more with recognizing *identity* than with the name per se.

Richardson then turns to how, historically, Christianity "lost its [missionary] zeal." He provides a strong, perhaps even scathing, criticism of how the Church utilized force and political power to enforce ecclesiastical unity and doctrinal uniformity. In these struggles, thus implemented, the Church lost its missionary zeal. This is why, according to Richardson, none of the early Christian creeds included the Great Commission.

I heartily recommend this book both as a challenge from a contemporary missionary statesman and as a biblical support for human decisions in missions.

Andrew C. Bowling, Ph.D.
Faculty Emeritus, John Brown University
Former faculty, Graduate Institute of Applied Linguistics (support person for Old Testament translation)
Published author (Old Testament studies and Biblical Hebrew)

1

IN THE CROSSHAIRS:
LOVE WINS AND *GOD WINS*

Rob Bell's Premise in *Love Wins*

Years ago, I met Rob Bell when he invited me to speak at Mars Hill Bible Church about God's mission to mankind. Rob was pastoring this growing church in Michigan. All these years later, my former acquaintance has authored *Love Wins: A Book About Heaven, Hell, and the Fate of Every Person Who Ever Lived*, in which he seeks to revoke the common understanding that the biblical hell is eternal. Unable to accept that God would subject anyone, let alone an assumed majority of mankind, to eternal torment, Rob Bell claims in *Love Wins*[1] that 100 percent of mankind will ultimately be saved.

Most writers who teach "universal salvation" simply disregard what the Bible says about hell. Rob Bell, conversely, accepts hell as real but views the punishment God administers there as *temporary*. Eventually, Bell believes, prolonged suffering in hell coerces every otherwise remorseless soul to repent, at which point, God invites them to join the festivities in heaven.

Bell seems to forget that anyone wise enough to know that a marathon stay in hell assures their eventual submission to God would also be wise enough to spare God the time, and themselves the pain, by repenting promptly.

It is also strange that Bell mentions salvation as ultimately assured for all of impenitent *humanity* only. What of Satan and the fallen angels? They, too, are sentient beings. Nowhere in *Love Wins* does Bell mention *their* eventual repentance as inevitable. This is a rather ironic omission. If he views God as justified in condemning *demons* to suffer eternally, Bell forfeits his base premise that divine love could not prescribe eternal suffering under *any* condition.

Like my former acquaintance, I, too, am concerned about holding a correct understanding of hell, daunting as the subject is. No other issue in the Bible has been more often castigated, ridiculed, feared, doubted, misunderstood or tweaked. Ultimately, every furor over hell turns, as in the title of Bell's book, on an assumed conflict between eternal punishment and the *love* of God.

Reasoning from Scripture?

On page 31, and again on page 91, in *Love Wins*, Rob Bell resurrects a ploy others before him have tried to offer as proof that hell will not flare eternally. He claims that the Greek term *aion* (the root of our English word "eon," sometimes spelled "aeon") refers to an indefinitely long age rather than eternity. Bell thus urges that *aion*, which he says is commonly mistranslated "eternal" in passages such as Matthew 25:46, actually describes the after-death affliction God imposes on unjust people as only a "period of pruning," a "time of trimming," that is, an intense but temporary "experience of correction."

Several reviewers take Rob Bell to task on his Greek semantics, especially because he misquotes the Greek text in Matthew 25:46. The Greek actually reads *Eis kolasin aionion* (εἰς κόλασιν αἰώνιον).[2] True, the Greek word *aionion* has *aion* as its root, but Greek scholars affirm that *aionion* clearly means "eternal" or "everlasting."[3] In Matthew 25:46, *aionion* defines the duration not only of "eternal punishment" but of "eternal life" as well. Thus, if hell is temporary, so is heaven. Try as he might, Bell cannot have *aionion* translated both ways.

Is Salvation a *Gift* or Coercion?

In *Love Wins*, Bell, in effect, claims that by granting finite beings the potential to hijack free will and wreak havoc, God obligates himself to save every havoc wreaker even if he must employ coercion. For those who reject it, salvation is thus no longer a gift, but an obligation ultimately imposed via pain.

What is so ironic here is that Bell, in a way, is almost right—the Bible *does* show hell as eliciting not repentance but a kind of stress-induced reformation. Consider the formerly aloof, self-obsessed rich man Jesus described in chapter 16 of Luke's Gospel. Confined to hell, despite intense discomfort, the rich man *pleads* with Abraham and Lazarus to help him. Far from demanding aid with cursing and blasphemy, he begs *politely* for minimal help. He also expresses concern that his five brothers be persuaded (not forced) to avoid his fate. He is changed already!

According to Rob Bell's intuition, this hell-incarcerated rich man—already reformed, already caring—was also already qualified for immediate transfer to heaven. Surely, God would "unfix" the intervening "chasm" between heaven and hell, and welcome him—a reformed sinner—to Paradise. But that is not how the narrative ends.

The apparent problem here, the real concern, is that a sinner's underlying sinful nature remains unchanged in hell however much attitudes and behavior may be improved due to stress. Thus, apart from an internal regeneration, rebels released from hell, relieved of the duress hell imposes, would not remain noble citizens for long, in which case, heaven—following their admittance—could not remain heavenly for long.

Jesus thus forewarns that hell actually accomplishes more than merely to repay sin with commensurate retribution. Most significantly, Jesus is depicting hell as rendering incarcerated beings—demons as well as humans, no doubt—incapable of performing any sinful act. By implication, were God to ease the duress needed to preempt not only evil acts but also evil intent, then lust, rage and even blasphemy would reemerge.

It follows that otherwise remorseless individuals, sustained in Hades at their respective thresholds of submission, rise as close to "peace" as they can ever come. Cartoon stereotypes lie to us. Demons wield no pitchforks in Hades. Even the devil himself, once incarcerated, will be as "subdued" as duress-induced submission can effect.

By contrast, earthly "penitentiaries," which generally fail to induce *penitence* in a majority of inmates, are misnamed. To the degree remorseless rapists, murderers, thieves, liars, abusers, terrorists and scam artists vent blasphemy and rage in their cells, earthly prisons fall far short of their eternal counterpart known as "hell."

All who repent while still alive—blessed by the birth of a new nature within—are freed at death from the evil nature that otherwise requires everyone to be subjected to stress. Eternal bliss ensues instead.

What Really Happens "Under the Earth"?

Lamentably, I recall hearing, years ago, a radio preacher opining that "hell will ring with blasphemy from end to end, forever!"

Actually, a far more reliable source describes another scene, wherein the responses are quite the opposite:

> *Every* knee should bow, in heaven and on earth and *under the earth*, and *every* tongue confess that Jesus Christ is Lord, to the glory of God the Father (Philippians 2:10-11, emphasis added).

Note that this will happen not only in heaven and even on earth, but—where else?—even *"under the earth,"* that is, in hell! I submit, therefore, that God's final judgment is designed to *suppress* sin as much as to *punish* it.

Will hosts of remorseless God-rejecters incarcerated in hell eventually shout, "Worthy is the Lamb who has forced us to love him by tormenting us for ages here in hell"? That would surely be an antithetical ending to this—the greatest epic ever—in which *persuasion*, despite its by-definition resistibility, triumphs over mere brute force.

Rather than eke out repentance from remorseless beings by force, God, at first, woos them to repent by encompassing them with necessarily resistible appeals. Later, according to Scripture, God justly *abandons* all who fail to respond in a timely manner, hence the warning:

> Seek the LORD while he may be found; call on him while he is near (Isaiah 55:6).

Justice that delays judgment forever is not justice. A time limit is obligatory.

How Mark Galli in His Book *God Wins* Responds to Rob Bell

Bell's misunderstanding of the Greek text is a major point examined by many reviewers. Yet Mark Galli, senior managing editor of *Christianity Today* magazine—critiquing Bell's views in his own book *God Wins*[4]—waits until his page 107 to discuss that key issue. Galli seems to accept Bell's comment that the key Greek term at issue is *aion* rather than *aionion*.

Curiously, Galli—who opposes Bell's attempt to redefine the biblical hell and frankly dubs Bell's universalism as "bad news"— still asks:

> Might God give people an opportunity to repent immediately after they die but before they are judged? We might hope this is true, especially for those who have never heard of Jesus, for example. But we simply are not told how God deals with such people.[5]

The problem with Galli's query is that everyone—blessed with the 20/20 hindsight an after-death experience affords—would shout a resounding "Yes!" if given a chance to repent after death. Then, of course, all need for hell as a repository for remorseless evildoers vanishes, unless hell is still required for demons only. So even Galli, merely by asking his rhetorical question, is actually positing that the universal salvation he denotes as "bad news" may somehow be what awaits impenitent mankind after death after all.

Galli adds, "We simply are not told" if such an option may exist. Yet Hebrews 9:27 frankly warns:

> Man is destined to die once, and after that to face judgment.

To find an intermediary second chance between death and judgment in that statement, one must argue from unwelcoming silence.

Expecting in advance (before reading his book) to find myself agreeing with so astute a fellow evangelical as Mark Galli, I am instead surprised at how freely he self-contradicts. Galli assures us that the Bible features "parable after parable about the final judgment and the eternal destruction of those who reject [God],"[6] adding:

> Not only did Jesus himself make these themes *central* to his teaching but he also is revealed to be the one through whom the judgment will finally take place. . . . God has *plainly revealed* to us that the Last Judgment and an eternal hell are realities that confront each of us [emphasis added].[7]

Yet, in his next paragraph, Galli appears to change his mind, sighing:

> But the Bible doesn't give us much beyond these few, bare truths. The exact nature of hell—fire? darkness? conscious torment? annihilation?—is not as clear.[8]

What more does Galli require? Specific temperatures and dimensions?

If, indeed, Jesus kept the theme of judgment "central to his teaching"—as Galli avers Jesus did in, for example, "parable after parable"—how could that strong a focus leave us with only "a few bare truths" to ponder? Either Jesus' teaching about hell is clear or it is vague. It can't be both. What Galli admits God has "plainly revealed" surely must also be plainly understandable.

Enough for now. I will return to Galli's analysis of the *Love Wins* quandary later.

Where Rob Bell Merits a Careful Response

In *Love Wins*, I do find one aspect of Rob Bell's objection to our common understanding of hell that merits a careful response. Pleading ever so plaintively against the *status quo* understanding of hell, Bell asks:

> Of all the billions of people who have ever lived, will only a select number "make it to a better place" and every single other person suffer in torment and punishment forever?[9]

Though I discount Bell's conclusion that hell is temporary rather than eternal, I agree with his opening premise that something is drastically wrong with the numerical factor. I refer here to the widespread Christian assumption that God is content to let Satan win in terms of dooming far more people made in God's image than Christ is able to save. When God's age-long war against evil ends, where will a majority of mankind be? In heaven, or in hell? The answer I develop in this book will, I suspect, surprise many.

2

WHY DID GOD "LEAVE A DOOR AJAR" FOR EVIL?

n my earliest writings—*Peace Child, Lords of the Earth,* and *Eternity in Their Hearts*—I acclaim the power of the glorious gospel of Jesus Christ to overcome evil, enabling even headhunters and cannibals to become people of Christlike character. Now, in *Heaven Wins,* I share my thoughts on three much more basic questions:

1. Why does evil have to exist only later to be overcome?
2. What does God gain by permitting and then overcoming evil, which would not otherwise be his?
3. How can it be that God calls people infected by evil—us— to join with him in his war against evil?

The Best Possible Cosmos?

Assuming that God's infinite knowledge foresaw a variety of creatable universes, why did he choose to create this one—a system in which evil would inevitably rise up to affront him? We tend to assume that a cosmos wherein God's goodness is never opposed would be super!

Yet, evidences embedded throughout the Bible explain why this cosmos is the one God chose. All of these evidences point to freewill response as so important to God that he would not bother to create even a single electron if free will would not be part of the outcome. It was a shockingly lonely experience for me to find at first that almost no one agreed with me that our wills have to be genuinely free for God's creation to be complete. That is why the late C. S. Lewis became like a special friend to me when I discovered years ago that he affirmed free will as corollary to the possibility of evil. Lewis made that point very clear in his book *Mere Christianity*:

God created things which had free will. . . . And free will is
what has made evil possible. Why, then, did God give them
free will? Because free will, though it makes evil possible, is
also the only thing that makes possible any love or goodness
or joy worth having. A world of automata—of creatures that
worked like machines—would hardly be worth creating.[1]

Nor could such be described as "made in God's likeness," as
James 3:9 affirms is our status.

In his book *The Screwtape Letters*, my new special friend added:

The irresistible and the indisputable are two weapons which
the very nature of His [God's] scheme forbids him to use.
Merely to override a human will . . . would be for him useless.
He cannot ravish. He can only woo.[2]

Enlarging upon these tenets that I find I share in common with
C. S. Lewis, I offer the following as an extension of them. I like to
think that what follows would please him.

Free Will:
An Inherently Double-edged Option

Possessing the option *not* to love God is what infuses our *choice* to
love him with such profound value—both for him and even for us!
For God to draw forth from finite beings that very real kind of love—a
kind that automatons could only mimic—the option for all finite
beings, both angelic and human, *not* to love God has to be made real
as well. That is why God has imparted to every finite citizen he has
created or will yet create an ability that mere denizens in fields and
forests, or in the deep, do not possess: the option to love God *or* turn
away from him!

What is it about free will that makes it of such paramount
importance to God? You might as well ask, "Why does a woman want
to have children?" Despite nine months of increasing discomfort
during gestation, the pain of childbirth and those early years of each
child's total dependence, she anticipates the pleasure of loving her
children and being loved and appreciated in return, even though

some children may disappoint! There are those who deem free will as incompatible with the supremacy of God. It's as if they want to protect God from the very thing he most supremely desires and is well-prepared to cope with.

So, then, God has chosen to endure the pain of rejection by some freewill beings for the sheer joy of loving and being loved by many more of the same.

Pleasure—Something Even an Infinite Parent Desires

I suggest that God's reason for creating this cosmos as opposed to any other is linked with something Scripture keeps assuring us is inherent to God's very nature. The Bible keeps portraying God as a Being who enjoys pleasure doing whatever he does! The *New International Version* of the Bible, from which I am citing texts throughout this treatise, ascribes no emphasis to any part of its text; so, emphasis added to any quote herein is my own. Thus, I will not keep repeating "emphasis added" when quoting Scripture.

The apostle Paul, in Ephesians 1:5, for example, speaks of God as working all things, not only according to his will, but according to "his *pleasure* and will."

Four verses later, Paul speaks of God's "good *pleasure*, which he purposed in Christ" (v. 9).

In Hebrews 12:2, the author of that epistle credits God the Son as One . . .

who for the *joy* set before him endured the cross, scorning its shame, and sat down at the right hand of the throne of God.

Paul affirms the following in 1 Corinthians 1:21:

God was *pleased* through the foolishness of what was preached to save those who believe.

So, then, what is the primary source of pleasure for God? In 1 John 4:8, we learn that "God is love."

Surely the God who *is* love desires not only to love but also to *receive* as much love as possible—love being the profoundest possible source of pleasure that is by nature true, good and enduring. Recurring analogies signifying Christ as the "bridegroom" and the true Church here on earth as "the bride, the wife of the Lamb" (Revelation 21:9) strongly emphasize the pleasure God finds by loving and being loved.

On the Other Side of Divine Emotion

Matthew 23:37 records that Jesus *wept* because of Jerusalem's intransigence. Dozens of other verses warn of attitudes and deeds that arouse God's wrath. God the Holy Spirit is described as one who can be *grieved* (see Ephesians 4:30).

These and many other passages impress upon us that God, far from being impassively and stoically aloof to the phenomenon of emotion, is himself a sublimely emotional Being in his own way and on a massive scale.

As redeemed people, we speak of experiencing "the *joy* of the Lord" and "the *peace* of God," often forgetting that these really are his emotions. Only as they originate in him does he freely bestow them to us.

Those Helpful "Omni-" Words

Centuries ago, theologians began coining "omni-" words to help us remember the various ways that God is infinite. We know, for example, that God is *omniscient* (all-knowing) as the sole possessor of infinite intellect. Scripture also affirms that God is *omnipotent* (all-powerful), the sole possessor of infinite will. And we know that God is also *omnipresent*—i.e., he occupies every point of space and every moment of time simultaneously.

Well and good! Yet could it be that we need to put a fourth "omni-" word into coinage, one that portrays God as sole possessor of a capacity to experience infinite, righteous emotion? Favoring that proposition, I suggest that God, whom we have for ages acknowledged as omniscient, omnipotent and omnipresent, possesses another infinite capacity that is just as awe-inspiring:

God Is Also Omni*sentient!*

The very thought amazes me. Why?

Having infinite knowledge is a static experience for God. A being who knows everything cannot add to his knowledge. Likewise an omnipotent being cannot make himself stronger. Yet God, by creating, is able to apply his infinite knowledge increasingly and utilize his infinite power multi-variously, provided he has a good enough reason to do so. And what might a good enough reason be?

As the Scriptures quoted earlier attest, God also has an infinite capacity to experience ever-heightening degrees of pleasure as he creates ever more beings to love and be loved by. And that, evidently, is what this cosmos is best able to afford.

If God were omniscient and omnipotent, but not omnisentient, why would the apostle Paul keep associating creation with God's pleasure? Surely it is because creation is designed and destined to satisfy God's infinite capacity to enjoy! Paul is adding another dimension to our view of creation and of God. Matter and energy exist merely to provide a setting for God to enjoy—to experience pleasure in—manifesting and receiving love.

The Problem of Percentages

If God foresaw that a *majority* of any number of freewill beings he might create would abuse free will by rebelling—thus needing eventually to be incarcerated—assumedly this universe would not exist at all, simply because the resulting pain would nullify God's just pursuit of pleasure. By that same token, this cosmos does exist, implying that God must have foreseen positive response from a sufficiently large majority of finite beings, including redeemed mankind. That is why the game is on! But wait! Thinking in terms of percentages of freewill responders versus rejecters suggests a game plan that God, of course, would have seen as exploitable. Let's huddle!

We have learned that mankind began with only two—Adam and Eve—but is steadily increasing by procreation. We tend to assume, however, that God created all the angels that will ever exist in one batch. Assuming that angels in that one batch do not procreate, the original angelic population remains constant forever. That would mean also that the percentages of angels who adore God versus those who rebelled will also remain fixed forever. What if that is not the whole story? What if God has a way to exploit the fall of a *minority* of angels in that first batch so as to guarantee that 100 percent of subsequent batches of angels will all remain loyal? That would surely alter the percentages in God's favor over time! Hmmm . . .

Please allow me to introduce a theory with a very strange name:

The Single Poignancy/Double Poignancy Theorem

What then determines how the ratio of angels who choose to honor their Creator versus those who rebel will fall out? Would not the ratio of freewill response versus rejection be proportional to how poignantly, how appealingly God is seen as worthy to be loved? Recall how Jesus in Luke 7:47 described factors such as mercy and forgiveness instilling feelings of greater or lesser degrees of poignant awe and love. So, the more intense the poignancy, the smaller will be the percentage of angels who rebel.

Imagine God creating that first host of angels for a "demo run." Newly self-aware, flexing both their ability to reason and their freedom to choose, they soon begin to ponder what they want their relationship with God to be like. Of course, their natural first response is one of awe and appreciation; but as time passes, a few begin to weigh another possibility. Unlike us, newly created angels did not have a nature already biased in favor of evil. Thus, whatever choice they made would be prompted solely by a freewill response to the goodness and glory of God as manifested in what?

Creation fully comprehended via general revelation is God's single poignancy persuasion!

That far back in time, creation was the only means God had to instill enough sufficiently poignant awe so as to win the love of those initial "demo run" angels. Munificent wonders filling billions of galaxies and the sublime unified field of truth undergirding it all—that became God's "single poignancy" persuasion.

Persuasions thus drawn from creation alone elicited a large-scale positive response, but it still fell short of 100 percent. Lucifer, exercising the option to reject God, persuaded others to join him in the first "falling away." Now for a crucial insight.

Were God to create still more batches of angels and keep offering them that same single-poignancy creation-based persuasion, similar percentages of rebels would keep recurring! God, however, knows better than to repeat the same test and expect a different result. That is why, before creating further hosts of freewill beings, God must first prepare an even more profound category of persuasions that, added to the "already there" magnificent appeal of creation, reduces the probability of rebellion amid yet-to-be-created angels all the way down to a beautiful, big, desirable *zero*!

How to Add an Even More Poignant Category of Persuasion

Rebellion by that small minority of "demo" angels was, of course, foreknown. God even foresaw and permitted the subsequent spread of their rebellion to us via our first parents as well. Above all else, God foresaw how poignantly his redemptive response to that initial abuse on behalf of fallen mankind would *limn, magnify, enhance* and *enrich* subsequent angelic and human perception of his wisdom and worth forever after!

Redemption fully comprehended via special revelation and added to the "already there" evidence of creation is what affords God with "double poignancy" persuasion. Double-poignancy persuasion is foreseen as guaranteeing 100 percent response from future hosts of freewill races God has yet to create on innumerable habitable planets cosmos-wide. And that is what assures God the pleasure of being worshiped, loved and praised by hosts of genuinely free finite beings, all without a single further abuse of freedom ever interrupting his and their mutual joy forever. Imagine this occurring on a scale so enormous as to be commensurate with the vastness of the universe itself. Apart from such a large-scale plan, what a *waste* of all that space waiting out there!

Centuries ago, when theology began to rise like a mist from the creeds, and then condense as doctrine, Christians thought creation consisted only of this world, the sun, the moon, an occasional comet, a few meteors and a mere 6,000 or so stars. And that seemed quite enough, thank you! Yet, all the while, the real scene has been billions of galaxies aswarm with giga-trillions of stars and undoubtedly innumerable habitable planets! Indeed, the first verse of the Bible declares that God created the "heavens" and the earth. The Hebrew word for "heavens" is significantly plural in number, *shamayim*, suggesting a plurality of galaxies, planets, and assorted phenomena. The New Testament also uses a plural form *ouranoi*, "heavens," suggesting the same thing. At the time of this writing, astronomers have already detected more than 760 planets orbiting around a considerably smaller number of stars just in our minuscule sector of the Milky Way—merely one galaxy among countless billions. Clearly, evidence is mounting that planets actually outnumber stars by far.

My double-poignancy theorem posits God as having a God-centered grand design commensurate with the scale of so vast a planet-filled cosmos, as depicted below:

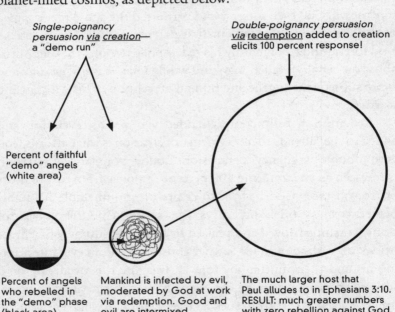

Single-poignancy persuasion *via creation*— a "demo run"

Double-poignancy persuasion *via* redemption added to creation elicits 100 percent response!

Percent of faithful "demo" angels (white area)

Percent of angels who rebelled in the "demo" phase (black area)

Mankind is infected by evil, moderated by God at work via redemption. Good and evil are intermixed.

The much larger host that Paul alludes to in Ephesians 3:10. RESULT: much greater numbers with zero rebellion against God.

With God's "demo run" completed, and redemption well under way, I posit God's vastly larger-scale operation as almost ready to be launched. Now that the supremely poignant story of God as Redeemer supplements the grand witness of God as Creator, what next? Consider God as ready now to populate billions of habitable planets across the cosmos with still more races of freewill beings—all with zero abuse of free will occurring ever again. That is a thought reminiscent of Psalm 102:18, though on a vastly larger scale:

> Let this be written for a future generation, that a people not yet created may praise the LORD.

All those future races, free of sin, will find their environments also free of disease, death and natural disasters. They will enjoy worlds that will be as this world would have been apart from the Fall. As Paul wrote:

> Creation was subjected to frustration [because of sin until the day when it] . . . will be liberated from its bondage to decay and brought into the glorious freedom of the children of God (Romans 8:20-21).

And Jesus, as part of his reward for coping sacrificially with the havoc wreaked upon heaven and mankind by that interfering initial minority of fallen "demo" angels, begins to reap more and more of "the joy set before him" (Hebrews 12:2). The poignant awe that future throngs of angels will feel while contemplating the real-time story of God incarnate pouring himself out to save fallen humans will surpass, by far, the creation-based persuasion that foreseeably failed to win a 100 percent response among the demo angels. After that:

> Of the *increase* of his government and peace there will be no end. . . . The zeal of the LORD Almighty will accomplish this (Isaiah 9:7).

To ensure clarity, I repeat the above thought reworded: God's judgment of fallen angels in the past and his response to the plight of fallen mankind on earth—when made known to yet-to-be-created hosts—will reveal God's wisdom, kindness and power so manifoldly that evil, initially permitted here for a demo purpose only, but subsequently contained in hell, will never recur across the entire cosmos forever.

Please observe how God-centered the above grand plan is! *His* glory and pleasure are the rightfully ultimate goal. Observe also what an honored part redeemed mankind fulfills. Born with evil embedded, we fall short of the glory of God, only subsequently to experience the power, joy and grace of redemption. Then, making the offer of salvation known to others, we heal the sick, comfort those who mourn, make peace, repay hatred with kindness and even suffer as martyrs, thanking our Lord for the privilege. All this to increase the awe, the profound amazement, of a story that will keep our yet-to-be-created younger brethren from repeating in the future what has happened in the past. And God—the Source and Sustainer of everything—enjoys a freewill-enhanced cosmos that at last is galvanized against evil forever.

Hints? Tips? Clues?

Do we, then, find hints, tips and even clues to such a grand plan enshadowed in Scripture? I believe we do—precisely where we discover Paul reveling over the "mystery" of God's "good pleasure" hidden in a plan that is yet . . .

> to be put into effect when the times will have reached their fullness [note Paul's emphasis on something new waiting to be unveiled in the future of the cosmos, something that requires ages to prepare]—to bring all things in heaven and on earth together under one head, even Christ (Ephesians 1:9,10).

This can only mean that evil, in due time, will not only be ultimately defeated but also ignominiously discredited and finally contained never to recur! And what exactly will be God's means of persuading yet-to-be-created citizens of God's cosmos never to exercise "the evil option" again? As Paul explains in Ephesians 2:7, God is at work now in order that "in the coming ages [note, not just "age"] he might show [show-case!] the incomparable riches of his grace, expressed in his kindness to us in Christ Jesus" [which, added to creation's witness, greatly heightens the poignancy].

I surmise that is exactly what Paul is also implying in Ephesians 3:10:

[God's] intent was that now, through the church, the manifold wisdom of God should be made known to the rulers
and authorities in the heavenly realms.

How noteworthy that Paul speaks of a plurality of "rulers," a
plurality of "authorities" in a plurality of "realms." Equally noteworthy is the adjective *manifold,* which Paul uses to designate a future
unveiling of multifaceted wisdom far greater than creation alone
could have attested to those long-ago, put-to-the-test "demo" angels.
No wonder hosts of redeemed people in heaven will one day cry that
not only creation but also "salvation belongs to our God . . . and to
the Lamb" (Revelation 7:10).

Again, Paul describes a great future unveiling of something very
grand having a profound effect upon the cosmos:

Creation waits in eager expectation for the sons of God to
be revealed (Romans 8:19).

With the witness of "salvation" profoundly paired with the prior
witness of creation, God's two greatest corollaries will be linked at last!

Some may ask, "Couldn't God just narrate a story of a fall that
led to redemption without having to let it all actually happen?"
Apparently even that would not have elicited a 100 percent response.
As we all know, real life is far more poignant than fiction.

God thus triumphs, not only justly but also in ways that discredit
evil so ignominiously that hosts of yet-to-be-created finite beings,
grasping the significance of "the manifold wisdom of God," will
reject the option of evil forever. I also think I detect the single-versus-
double-poignancy theorem beckoning to us from one of our Lord's
most intriguing parables.

The "Price" an *Omnisentient* God
Was Willing to Pay

As Jesus explained by way of a parable recorded in Matthew 13:44-46,
God, weighing options, *invested!* Choosing to pay a price required,

he "bought the whole field" of creation for the sake of "a hidden treasure" he knew he would find ensconced within. What else could that treasure be than the love he desires from genuinely free finite beings, a love offered to him by choice rather than involuntarily or by coercion? And this is to happen despite the equally real option they all possess—the option not to love him.

That love is the "pearl of great price" and the "treasure hidden in a field" that it became God's pleasure to pay for and to genuinely possess. But what is the "price" God must pay to truly own the hidden "pearl" in this vast but oh-so-strategic "field" we call the cosmos? By coping self-sacrificially with the abuse wreaked by a small initial minority, God persuasively and justly secures the loyalty of much larger hosts for the rest of eternity.

Great deal!

That is why it was, after all, wise for God to create a cosmos with a door left ajar for evil. Desiring the pleasure of loving and being loved is innate to personhood—God's as well as ours (since we are created in his likeness).

Apart from receiving love offered by freewill beings, why create? God does not need matter to survive. Matter and energy exist merely to serve as a habitat for responsive freewill beings who love God. To assure that 100 percent of yet-to-be-created hosts will exploit their freedom of choice with zero abuse forever, God is inviting us— infected with evil though we are—to rally to his side. The fact that we struggle against evil, though infected by it, ramps up the poignancy of the great story.

What a crucible of a world our home planet is! Here, with God's help, we must struggle to manifest the best use of free will that we can manage, while many around us waste the same precious gift for its very worst potential. And all the while, God, through us, is preparing a lesson of ultimate potency to benefit giga-trillions of our future fellow-citizens across the widest extents of time and space.

Jesus, in the Great Commission, appointed us to be his "witnesses in Jerusalem, and in all Judea and Samaria, and to the ends of the earth" (Acts 1:8). In this world, we witness for him to persuade people for whom he died to turn from sin to God. What I foresee is a Great Commission Phase II, in which we as redeemed

WHY DID GOD "LEAVE A DOOR AJAR" FOR EVIL?   33

earthlings, merely by narrating our story, persuade newly created freewill beings not to turn from God to sin. And that is a witness destined to sweep us far past the ends of this one planet to Orion, Pegasus, Andromeda and points beyond.

The more this, my heartfelt theory, is greeted with disbelief, the more I hope one day to shout a triumphant, "I told you so!" out there among the stars.

That, then, is why evil had to be allowed to make a brief appearance only later to be overcome. We also see what God gains by overcoming evil he permitted to appear that could not otherwise be his apart from permitting it to appear and then overcoming it. I have also expressed how people infected by evil—us—enabled by God's grace, can bring glory to God by striving against evil within and without via the atoning sacrifice God himself made for us. And this is just the threshold to a fuller understanding of how *Heaven Wins!*

A Cosmic Lesson from an Ancient Book

The book of Job provides a stirring example of God accomplishing what is described above—using someone infected with evil to overcome evil while hosts of angels observe. Why does God desire that angels watch something as poignant as Job's struggle against his own potential to rebel against God? Observe that Job vindicated God on the basis of creation's single-poignancy persuasion, putting to shame the angels for whom that persuasion was not enough.

Please try to grasp why this matter of poignancy is so crucial to God, because you are meant to be a source of it yourself!

As the Bible avers throughout, God desires to win love from finite beings by profound persuasion. Not by coercion or force. Persuasion, by definition, has to be resistible, else persuasion is simply force renamed. This brings us to a trenchant issue that the book of Job, thought to be the Bible's first written treatise, raises in its opening chapter.

The book of Job opens with Satan insinuating—amid a host of angels assembled presumably from already inhabited nearby parts of the cosmos—that not even a man as righteous as Job genuinely credits God as meriting unsolicited love. Satan slurs the integrity of the Almighty by accusing God of bribing "love" from Job via the artifice of catering to Job's greed!

Does Job love God for nothing? (See Job 1:9.)

Satan then gloats:

> Take back everything you gave to him and he will curse you!
> (v. 11).

Is Satan right? Is greed—spawned by Satan but resident now in human nature as well—a flaw that even God must acknowledge so as to be "loved" by mankind? If so, Job's "love" for God is nothing more than a flawed response mitigated by Satan. Satan, a finite being, thus in this one sense may claim victory over God in a cosmos-wide ongoing contest. If, in fact, the Almighty must bow to an attribute of evil so as to be loved by mankind, *Satan wins!*

Like nothing else in all of space and time, Satan's taunt is one that God, in the presence of "such a great cloud of witnesses" (Hebrews 12:1), must not ignore. If God does not somehow refute Satan's taunt, will other as-yet-loyal angels be induced to join Satan's rebellion? Suspense grips the angelic host as God hands over to Job, a mere mortal, the direst responsibility and highest honor a finite being can ever shoulder—a chance to summon the will before an agog cosmos to prove that a mere man can genuinely love God *simply because God is God!*

Such a Traumatic Test!

Suddenly bereaved of children and possessions—all with God's consent—Job . . .

> fell to the ground in worship and said: . . . "The LORD gave and the LORD has taken away; may the name of the LORD be praised" (Job 1:20).

Hosts of holy angels cheer, tossing haloes aloft! Satan groans. *Heaven wins!*

Century by century, saga after saga, the same persuasively

poignant vision unfolds and expands until God himself, vulnerably incarnated, declares:

> I, when I am lifted up from the earth, will *draw* [not drag or coerce or force] all men to myself (John 12:32).

Thus does God himself, lifted up to bleed and die for us on a cross, draw us by poignantly atoning for our sin. Do not persuasions surpassingly more poignant than those known to Job illumine us today? If a man of his long-ago age, lacking the subsequent revelations God has arrayed before us, could avow God as inherently worthy before a watching cosmos, then how much more ought we to attest the God who has saved us as utterly worthy of our love now?

Peter the apostle states in his first letter that angels still ponder the cosmically significant struggle between good and evil yet being waged on this unique arena planet (see 1 Peter 1:12). And the writer of the letter to the Hebrews, echoing what Job and Peter reveal about angelic attentiveness to earthly issues, counsels:

> Surrounded by such a great cloud of witnesses [angels included!], . . . let us run with perseverance the race marked out for us (Hebrews 12:1).

Ultimately, at an epic celebration foreseen in the Apocalypse, praise will erupt from the throats of "thousands upon thousands, and ten thousand times ten thousand" of sublimely, poignantly, awesomely persuaded finite beings who shout:

> *Worthy* is the Lamb, who was slain! (Revelation 5:11-12)

God Has Paid *His* Price;
Those Who Rebel Must Also Pay *Theirs*

As for the minority of angels who abused the freedom God granted, they too must pay a price for evil, in their case as its original perpetrators. Justly and forever they are yet to be both incarcerated and incapacitated in hell.

Now, as we segue from the way a majority of the angels chose to honor God at the beginning, and the anticipated unanimity of yet-to-be-created populations throughout the cosmos, what about mankind here on earth? Is the God who won in terms of the sheer number of holy angels who remained faithful destined to lose a majority of mankind despite the sacrifice of Christ on our behalf?

Granting God his obvious *moral* victory over evil, when it comes to a tally of actual numbers, will Satan be able to claim that he has defeated God by dooming far more people made in God's image than Jesus will have been able to save via his atoning death and resurrection?

Unlike the holy angels, each of us begins life with the sinful nature we automatically inherit from Adam already embedded within us—a serious liability, to be sure. Does that liability guarantee doom for a majority of mankind? It seems that a majority of Christians grimly accept the notion that, yes, a majority of humanity is indeed lost and doomed.

I disagree. Let me explain why.

DOES A MERELY *PYRRHIC* VICTORY OVER EVIL BEFIT GOD?

A Pyrrhic victory is a triumph offset by staggering loss. Picture a king who wins a battle only to discover that a mere pittance of his subjects remain alive after the struggle. Yes, his enemies, duly defeated, flee the field of battle; but they are slaughtering thousands of his citizens and kidnapping others as they retreat!

A Pyrrhic victory, then, can also be a moral triumph discredited by grievous statistical loss. With that possibility in mind, will God's ultimate victory over evil end up morally resplendent but numerically ignominious?

Paul the apostle asserts that God has achieved a glorious victory over Satan and the demons in that he,

> having disarmed the powers and authorities . . . made a public spectacle of them, triumphing over them by the cross (Colossians 2:15).

So—will God's momentous triumph over evil be both moral *and* numerical? Or will the powers of evil, despite being "disarmed" by the cross, somehow achieve a statistical triumph over Almighty God by dooming far more bearers of God's image than Christ is able to save? If that happens, will not God's assured moral victory over Satan be left looking tragically *Pyrrhic*? When Paul's paraphrase of Hosea 13:14 rings out for the final time, "Where, O death, is your victory?" (1 Corinthians 15:55), will the lord of death be able to quip, "Look at the numbers"?

That would hardly fit with Jesus' promise that "the gates of hell will not overcome [the Church he is building]" (Matthew 16:18).

Amazingly, millions of Christians who credit God as morally victorious over evil at the cross rather mindlessly (it seems to me) credit a statistical triumph to the forces of hell. In their view, heaven ends up resembling a mere "village," whereas hell, in terms of human occupants, becomes a teeming, albeit thoroughly chaotic, "metropolis." As cited earlier, it is in fact this tragic outcome that Rob Bell, in *Love Wins*, pleads against ever so plaintively, asking:

> Of all the billions of people who have ever lived, will only a select number "make it to a better place" and every single other person suffer in torment and punishment forever?[1]

Whereas Rob Bell voices his protest from within the Evangelical movement, unbelievers around us also object bitterly that what they see as our exclusive Christian elitism smugly bans a majority of mankind from heaven.

If this is truly an integral part of the inevitable "offense of the cross," we Christians must simply bear it. But let's be sure.

Though Bell's universal salvation is the wrong answer to this grim "quantities quandary," still, I believe that Rob Bell's intuition that God should not have to claim a moral victory over evil at the cost of a statistical defeat is correct.

Mark Galli Again

On an opposite side of this same issue, the idea that God would settle for a *de facto* Pyrrhic victory over evil is something Mark Galli—in his ironically titled book *God Wins*—dismisses as inconsequential. Galli writes:

> Though we should care about the fate of the unsaved, the matter of how many are saved or are not saved doesn't have to be a concern of ours. We can put that matter into the hands of a good and wise Savior.[2]

We don't need to put that matter in God's hands. It is already there. But the fact that something rests in God's hands does not *ipso facto* partition it apart from human concern and curiosity.

Obviously, if God is willing to settle for a Pyrrhic victory over evil, that is God's right. My concern is that we are guilty of wrongly inferring a Pyrrhic victory for God without his consent, that is, without biblical basis.

I believe Rob Bell genuinely cares about how many people are saved versus how many are lost. So do I. I warrant that so does Mark Galli, if he would search his heart for a moment. Most important, Scripture reveals that numbers of people matter to God as well. God rebuked Jonah for grieving the loss of one vine over against God's victory in delivering 120,000 people in Nineveh from judgment (see Jonah 4:11).

God cares about and even *counts* human populations! Yet Galli opines:

> A billion people is to the Lord as one, and one person as to a billion. How God . . . manages the population of heaven is not something we can possibly understand.[3]

The latter part of Mr. Galli's rather odd comment would be factual except that God has seeded the Bible with eye-opening, out-in-the-open clues as to how his guaranteed moral victory over evil guarantees a statistical victory for heaven as well.

If both Bell and Galli would simply ponder the fact of mankind's age-long high infant mortality phenomenon and compare that fact with what the Bible says about the status of children before God, perhaps these two authors would begin to change their minds about the eternal destiny of this large majority of mankind. Instead, incoherent thinking about a hazily explained "age of accountability" characterizes almost all Christians everywhere.

Raise the subject of an "age of accountability" in conversation with Christians and eyes will generally glaze over. Of course, on the other hand, some pastors or priests coldly warn everyone that God excludes all unbaptized babies and even improperly baptized babies from heaven.

Rob Bell himself, in a mildly sarcastic tone, ridicules the idea of an "age of accountability."[4] Bell seems to have no awareness or concern as to whether the Bible supports the concept or not. Even Mark Galli, the leading evangelical scholar I quoted earlier, unapologetically questions whether there is any such thing as an "age of accountability." He queries:

> What about those who die as infants or children and don't have an opportunity to respond in faith to Christ?[5]

Galli, replying to Galli, opines:

> We so desperately want to answer these questions, but the fact is that God has not revealed what he will or will not do in these cases.[6]

Well, now, that is strange, because I hear pastors assure congregants who lose a child that their little one is in heaven. Many pastors, at least when put on the spot, assure even bereaved unbelievers that their child who died is in God's arms. Well and good! Longing to go where a beloved child has already gone may persuade an occasional unbeliever to turn to Jesus and be saved himself.

So—if Mr. Galli's claim that God hasn't told us what happens to children who die is correct, all such pastors who assure the bereaved as to where their deceased child is must be either uninformed or speaking tongue in cheek. Or are they adapting their theology to cater to the audience of the moment?

So, then, may we, or may we not, confidently believe that every child who dies prior to a moment of accountability—whenever that is—is saved? I find that most of my many Bible-believing friends assume that, yes, we may so believe. If so, why don't we all apply what we say we believe about children who die here and now, where we live, to the billions of other children who have been dying everywhere else in the world in every age even up till now?

And if, indeed, the Bible does aver that all who die as children are saved, shouldn't that belief be deemed important enough to list among our doctrines and at least mention, if not preach, on occasion from the pulpit?

Shouldn't we begin advising unbelievers who have lost a little one, saying, "All who yearn to see a deceased infant again—whether that be a child, grandchild, niece, nephew or friend—repent and turn to Jesus; he has all your deceased little ones under his care. Submit yourselves under his rule as your Lord and Savior and you will meet them again. And what is more, that blessed reunion will happen *in his presence!*"

By disparaging an age of accountability as wishful thinking, Bell and Galli unwittingly clear a platform for me to refute their views, with a degree of help from others. Together, we will prove that the Bible truly does reveal what happens to children who die prior to knowing enough to render themselves culpable before God.

IS THE BIBLE REALLY VAGUE ABOUT AN "AGE OF ACCOUNTABILITY"?

Granted, what happens to all who die in childhood is not a major theme throughout the Bible. God's primary concern in Scripture is to bring those of us who survive early death to saving faith and productive spiritual maturity as citizens of his kingdom. Those who believe that mankind is subject to "doom from the womb to the tomb" (apart from infant baptism, in some systems of belief) are prone to quote Scriptures such as the following:

> Even from birth the wicked go astray; from the womb they are wayward and speak lies (Psalm 58:3).

This, however, has to be Davidic hyperbole; newborns can neither walk nor talk. It was this same David who also wrote in Psalm 8:2:

> From the lips of children and infants you have ordained praise.

Our Lord himself quoted Psalm 8:2 in Matthew 21:16.

David also saw himself as "sinful at birth, sinful from the time my mother conceived me" (Psalm 51:5). In New Testament phraseology, that translates to being conceived with an Adamic nature.

Other Christians agree with Rob Bell and Mark Galli that the Bible is actually *silent* regarding the destiny of children who die. A majority seem to feel that it is not so much silent on the topic, but *vague*. In fact, the Bible is neither silent nor vague on this extremely important topic. Evidence abounds.

What the Old Testament Reveals
About the Status of Children

Denouncing Israel for a rebellion in the Sinai desert, God demarcated different degrees of accountability vis-à-vis adults and children with the following warning in the book of Deuteronomy:

> Not a man of this evil generation shall see the good land I swore to give your forefathers [but] . . . your children who do not yet know good from bad—they will enter the land (Deuteronomy 1:35,39).

The book of Isaiah also introduces the basic concept of a moment of accountability as if hinting that it may have theological significance:

> Before the boy knows enough to reject the wrong and choose the right (Isaiah 7:16).

But King David, centuries earlier, had already avowed that the soul of a certain deceased infant was already in heaven. Concerning his infant son who had just died, David said:

> I will go to him, but he will not return to me (2 Samuel 12:23).

The Four Gospels and the Status of Children

Some rigorist Christians quote Matthew 7:14 and 22:14 as evidence that God is not at all concerned if more people, including deceased children, are lost than are saved, despite all he has done at such great cost to provide salvation. In Matthew 7:14 and 22:14 respectively, Jesus said:

> Small is the gate and narrow the road that leads to life, and only a few find it.

> Many are invited, but few are chosen.

Of course, Jesus was speaking, in both passages, of people old enough to understand a call and comprehending enough to know that salvation is something they are both able and responsible to "seek" and even "find." Unborn infants or young children (some of whom can hardly find their own noses) do not fit at all within the scope of Jesus' Matthew 7:14 and 22:14 comments.

Rigorists who apply the above two quotes from Matthew to represent God as unwilling to save as many people as possible are disregarding other parts of God's Word where we read, for example, that God is "not wanting *anyone* to perish, but everyone to come to repentance" (2 Peter 3:9).

This, by the way, is not the same as declaring, as Rob Bell does, that everyone will repent.

Still, the mere fact that down through the ages a large *majority* of mankind has died in childhood surely warrants mention of an "age of accountability" somewhere in Scripture, assuming God himself sees the topic as vital. He does!

We find Jesus himself affirming a blessed bond with children via various comments. In Matthew 18:3, he warned:

Unless you change and become like little children, you will never enter the kingdom of heaven.

In Matthew 18:10, Jesus cautioned:

See that you do not look down on . . . these little ones. For I tell you that their angels in heaven always see the face of my Father in heaven.

In Matthew 19:14, Mark 10:14 and Luke 18:16 (that is, in all three synoptic Gospels), Jesus urged:

Let the little children come to me . . . for the kingdom of heaven belongs to such as these.

If the kingdom of heaven actually belongs to little children, where do we suppose little children are destined to go if they die as little children? Is it really difficult to conclude that they are destined to go to a place where they belong and which even belongs to them?

Pondering the above five texts from three Gospels, one begins to sense that salvation really is guaranteed for children up to a certain age.

How can it be, then, that many Christians—despite King David's comment about his deceased child and the above five texts from all three synoptic Gospels—still demur by preferring to view belief in an age of accountability as *an option*, at best, but certainly not as a doctrine? Every theologian and even a large majority of devout lay Christians know about these Scripture verses. Millions of us have even memorized some of them!

I think I know the answer. Devout Christians, at least tacitly, believe that every teaching that is *primary* in the Old Testament and in the Gospels invariably shows up *affirmed* by at least one apostle in at least one epistle. So, the assumption goes, if an Old Testament tenet or even a *"Gospel* truth" cannot be found in at least one epistle, it remains true, yes, but somehow only on a lower level than Church doctrine.

That is my theory.

I'm guessing that is why Mark Galli, for example—despite being fully aware of all of the above texts—would still infer that "God has not revealed" what happens to children who die before responding to the gospel.

Based on my supposition, of course, I must turn now to the Epistles where—to my knowledge—the proposition that Christ's atonement covers every child from conception until his or her moment of accountability thus far remains theologically unconfirmed, at least in biblical commentaries!

If indeed Paul, Peter, James and John actually leave the hopeful proposition of an age of accountability unconfirmed in their letters, it is to be assumed that the Church will forever regard belief in it as optional. So—can this longstanding *status quo* be changed? Must belief in an age of accountability remain as it has until now—an undercover tenet demoted to the cellars of Christian thought?

Virtually everyone who reads what follows may at some point need to comfort a friend who has lost a child or may need to be comforted for the same loss. I pray the following presentation of scriptural truth will be of help at such a time.

What Do the Epistles Say?

Theologians agree that Paul typified himself as representing mankind when he declared in Romans 7:9:

> Once I was **alive** apart from the law; but when the commandment came, sin sprang to life and I **died**.

Paul literally avers that he, as a child, remained *spiritually* alive as long as the sinful nature he inherited from Adam lay dormant within him. Paul did not "die" spiritually until that sinful nature, once activated, seduced him. And that, of course, could not happen until he had aged enough to comprehend a given act as engendering moral culpability.

Thus every human being, like Paul, also remains spiritually alive as long as the sinful component of the Adamic nature remains dormant. Apparently Christ's self-sacrifice atones for the mere *presence* of our sinful nature as long as it remains dormant. That said, it follows that every individual is free from divine condemnation from conception until at least the first few years of life. Thus, children who die while their sinful nature remains *dormant* die uncondemned and enter heaven free from sin forever.

Paul affirms the same point in 2 Corinthians 5:10, explaining that mankind is judged, not because of Adam's sin but according to each individual's record of "things *done* while in the body, whether good or bad." Likewise the apostle John clarifies in Revelation 20:13 that "each person [will be] judged according to what he had *done*." Adding to Paul's and John's warnings against "sins of commission," James 4:17 warns that there are also "sins of omission," saying:

> Anyone, then, who knows the good he ought to do and doesn't do it, sins.

Despite the above clarifications, rigorist Christians claim it makes no difference if children die while the Adamic nature is still dormant; God condemns them merely because the Adamic nature is *in* them. If the apostle Paul agreed with that view, surely he would have worded Romans 3:23 as follows: "Everyone conceived with a sinful nature is denied the glory of God." Instead, Paul penned:

All have *sinned* and fall short of the glory of God.

One cannot "fall short" of the glory of God by sinning unless one already possesses a mercifully endowed right of access to the glory of God prior to sinning! Paul, in Romans 3:23, thus astutely affirms that one's first consciously willful aberrant *deed* is what precipitates lostness.

Who was Paul designating by the word "all" in Romans 3:23?

Aware that anyone reading his words with comprehension will be someone who, like Paul himself, has already emerged from childhood innocence by sinning, Paul's "all" obviously does not include billions of deceased children who did not live long enough to "fall short of the glory of God." Paul's "all" in Romans 3:23 thus includes only the surviving portion of mankind—those of us who, by sinning, have become spiritually dead and must repent and believe to enter the kingdom of God.

Still More Evidence Abounds in Paul's Writings!

Two verses after Romans 7:9, Paul reiterates his Romans 7:9 transition from a state of "life" to one of spiritual "death" *again*, still with no hint of figurative meaning. As Paul explains in Romans 7:11, his sinful nature, "seizing the opportunity afforded by the commandment, deceived me, and through the commandment put me to death."

By inference, had Paul died *physically* prior to that destiny-altering moment, an automatic "safety clause," so to speak—afforded by our Lord's sacrifice of himself—would have opened heaven's door for little Paul just as it did for David's deceased infant centuries before. And all of this would have transpired despite a dormant sinful nature and youthful ignorance of divine revelation.

Visiting Paul again, in 1 Corinthians 15:22, we find him reaffirming his teaching in Romans. Note his wording:

For as in Adam all *die*, so in Christ all will be made alive.

Paul did not say, "as in Adam all *are dead*." If he had, we would conclude that to be conceived as a descendant of Adam is to be "dead in Adam" concurrently. But in Paul's actual comment, "die" is a verb designating an *event* that transitions one from "being alive" to "being dead." One cannot "die in Adam" apart from first being *alive despite the Adamic nature*. Without a doubt, 1 Corinthians 15:22 affirms spiritual death as ensuing only when the nature imparted to us from Adam becomes activated, resulting in actual sin in real time.

Something Paul wrote in Romans 5:12 adds still more confirmation:

> Sin entered the world through one man, and death through sin, and in this way death came to all men *because all sinned*.

Again and again, Paul is consistently describing spiritual death as precipitated by an actual *act* of sin in real time. But what comprises an act of sin by a child? I heard one parent exclaim, "A newborn baby can scream and rage, and that is sin." I wanted to ask, "Are you actually able to read a newborn baby's mind?" If that or any similar charge were true, that is, if babies are condemned to hell because they scream, Jesus misspoke when he said that the kingdom of heaven belongs to little children (see Matthew 19:14).

Though knowledge is not prerequisite to being born with a sinful nature, it is prerequisite to any sinful act; and as we have learned from Paul's teaching, it takes a sinful act to precipitate condemnation. And even when a child understands a command, if he honestly tries to ascertain the logic behind the command prior to obeying it, I submit that he is not actually disobeying the command itself.

When one of my sons was about four years old, I warned him not to play on the street because a car might come around the corner and run over him. The command made perfectly good sense to me, but it aroused in my son a new curiosity. Later, he came into the house and cheerfully informed me, "Daddy, I went out and laid down in the road and I didn't get runned over!" I was sure that his determination to prove me wrong had inspired him to look both ways very carefully before lying down on the street. I saw his action as an honest experiment rather than an act of defiance, and no discipline ensued. With his experiment behind him, he willingly obeyed my prohibition against playing out on the street.

Our purpose here is not to determine when a child's age of accountability ensues, but rather to show from Scripture that until that moment, every child is covered by the sacrifice of Christ and goes to heaven should he or she die while still in that state.

Paul infers an age of accountability again in Ephesians 2. He advises Gentile converts that they became spiritually dead only when the sinful nature they inherited at conception ceased to be dormant. Spiritual death ensued—as in Romans 7:9—not due to a dormant sinful nature but due only to an *activated* sinful nature! Note Paul's point:

> As for you, you were dead *in your transgressions and sins* (Ephesians 2:1).

Four verses later, Paul infers an age of accountability again in Ephesians 2:5. This time he even includes himself, a Jew, as sharing a common past with former pagans in Ephesus. Paul wrote:

> Even when *we* were dead in transgressions.

Observe that in both passages Paul links spiritual death with actual *transgressions* committed following childhood, obviously, rather than concurrent with conception.

Paul infers an age of accountability in yet another passage— Colossians 2:13—with an added comment this time:

> When you were dead *in your sins* and in the uncircumcision
> of your sinful nature, God made you alive with Christ.

An *activated* sinful nature—once it has prompted a person to sin and die spiritually—of course *remains* activated within him; hence Paul accurately describes sinners who are already spiritually dead as dead both because of actual sins *and* their sinful nature.

As for the scourge of abortion, God will scourge impenitent aborters according to his sixth commandment, but receives into his presence the infants they slay.

Rigorist Christians often quote a bromide crediting the Adamic nature as subjecting mankind to "doom from the womb to the tomb." Measured against the above array of texts, that ghastly utterance is at last fully exposed as devoid of biblical basis despite its clever rhyme.

There we have it. Romans 7:9 and 7:11, linked with all these other Pauline texts cited, constitute solid theological basis for Christians to honor the concept of an "age of accountability" as confirmed in the Epistles as well as elsewhere in Scripture.

Why, then, have we not heard these many other proofs taught this way before? One major historical barrier to the above straightforward understanding of the above textual array traces back to Augustine of Hippo's overstated definition of total depravity. I will deal summarily with Augustine later in this treatise, but first let me explain a related objection that still rankles in theological circles.

How Dare Anyone *Compete* with Adam and Eve!

Down through the centuries, the Church has assumed that Adam and Eve are unique as the only human beings to fall from being spiritually alive to being spiritually dead. Assumedly we, their progeny, have to make that transition solely *in the reverse direction*, i.e., from being spiritually dead back to being spiritually alive. Accepting that Paul, as a child, could fall from spiritual life to spiritual death pits him as competing in a sense with our first parents, contrary to the Church's long-standing assumption about our first parents.

There are three key differences between Adam and Eve on one hand and Paul and the rest of us on the other:

1. Adam and Eve were spiritually alive with no guarantee that spiritual death would overtake them at a given moment. We, as their progeny, are spiritually alive in a Romans 7:9 sense but only on a provisional, temporary basis.

2. Our sin is *abetted* when a dormant sinful nature uncoils and strikes *within* us, whereas Eve and Adam—while still pure—yielded to a temptation abetted by an *external* tempter.

3. The assertion that we all die in Adam remains true even if each of *us* actually replicates Adam's fall from life to

death. Our individual fallings do not mark the onset of a new multigenerational infection such as Adam initiated.

Looking back into church history, we find the earliest church fathers affirming that deceased children are welcomed into the presence of God.

How a Serious Mental Block Originated

As an example of very early opinion about the fate of deceased children, we have Irenaeus, a second-century Church Father. Speaking of Herod's slaughter of the infants in Bethlehem described in Matthew 2:16-18, Irenaeus saw that tragedy as overruled by Christ, who:

> Suddenly removed those children belonging to the house of David, . . . that he might send them on before into his kingdom; he, since he was himself an infant, so arranging it that human infants should be martyrs, slain, according to the Scriptures, for the sake of Christ, who was born in Bethlehem of Judah, in the city of David.[1]

> Who are they that have been saved and received the inheritance? Those, doubtless, who do believe God, and who have continued in his love . . . *and innocent children, who have had no sense of evil.*[2]

A century or two later, a British monk, Pelagius, opposed the doctrine of original sin as promulgated by Augustine of Hippo. Pelagius wrongly posited that when Adam sinned, only Adam was affected. All children thereafter are born with no sinful nature at all, let alone an initially dormant one inherited from Adam.

Though Pelagius gained many followers in Rome, his teachings were rightly judged as anti-biblical. However, by the time Augustine had defeated Pelagius with exaggerations of his own, mankind's condemnation was no longer deemed as *concurrent with one's first act of sin but as concurrent with conception itself.*

Though Pelagius misrepresented Scripture in many ways, Augustine also, while defending the doctrine of human depravity, took the Church beyond Scripture. Pondering Paul's Ephesians 2:1 reference to mankind as "dead in transgressions and sins," Augustine, who spoke Latin, thought he understood what Paul was signifying by using the Greek term *nekros* (Greek νεκρός—*"dead"*) relative to the condition of unregenerate people.

What Happens at the Moment of Physical Death?

First, some important background: Two primary events occur at death. First and foremost, the living soul *separates* from the body, from loved ones and from the world. Second, once the soul is gone, *bodily functions cease*. A cautious interpreter of Ephesians 2:1 should of course ask which of these two "death events" best fits Paul's analogy linked with *nekros*. The first? The second? Both?

A word search to see how Paul and other New Testament persons used analogies drawn from *nekros* or other Greek terms for death was obviously warranted. If Augustine had done a careful word search—one that I will in fact trace in a later chapter—he would have found strong indication that *separation from God* rather than *cessation of function* signifies what Paul and other New Testament writers meant when using *nekros* analogously.

But, consistent with his belief that cessation of function explains Paul's analogy, from the time of his debate with Pelagius, Augustine famously began declaring that mankind is so spiritually dead as to be "unable even to *incline* toward what is good." Ergo, from that time forward, Christians who previously agreed that mankind is "depraved" began to insist that mankind is "*totally* depraved"!

Though all sinners are indeed "dead" by virtue of their separation from God, they retain the ability—like the Prodigal Son (also described by his father as "dead")—to choose to repent. It is far and away plightful enough that we human beings cannot free ourselves from sin, cannot atone for our sin, cannot save ourselves and cannot rid ourselves of the Adamic nature. Adding to these innate "cannots" by claiming that we lack all ability even to *rue* our lost condition was unjustified and misleading.

In his early adulthood, Augustine belonged to the Manichæan cult, a group who defined the physical human body as totally evil. Did Augustine simply transfer a latent Manichæan urge to aver something as totally evil from the human body to the human spirit?

Why a Theological Ruse Was Needed

Siding with Augustine's view of depravity as "total," and the Church's assumption that none other than Adam and Eve fell from life to death, Christian scholars have been loath to posit mankind's Adamic nature as passively *dormant* at any stage, let alone *uncondemned* at any moment.

Aghast lest Paul be seen as contradicting Augustine on total depravity, otherwise consistent scholars had to devise a way to bring Paul's perfectly clear teaching in passages like Romans 7:9, Romans 7:11 and the many other concurring passages cited earlier into conformity with the Church's *status quo* assumptions about Adam and Eve and Augustine's new theology. Scholars virtually en masse began insisting that Paul's Romans 7:9 statement must be understood *figuratively* rather than literally, as if Paul meant to say, "Once, in a certain sense, I was 'alive' apart from the law, but when the commandment came, sin sprang to life and, in a certain sense, 'I died.'"

Elsewhere, when Paul intends us to understand him subjectively, he forewarns us to understand him subjectively. Again and again, Paul introduces distinctively subjective teaching with phrases like these:

Let me take an *example* from everyday life (Galatians 3:15).

These things may be taken *figuratively* (Galatians 4:24).

These are a *shadow* of . . . things . . . to come (Colossians 2:17).

Yet, Paul attaches not even one such indication of subjective meaning to any of the above quotes, every one of which shows Paul defining sin committed in real time as precipitating human lostness. I submit that a literal understanding of Roman 7:9 is thus vindicated. Yet over the centuries, each generation of Christian scholars has insistently impressed a subjective understanding of Romans 7:9 upon the next generation. For example, note the following quote from the 1700s.

Matthew Henry on Romans 7:9

Matthew Henry, who died in 1714, was one of the first commentators to draft, at least for modern readers, the following exegesis of what Paul supposedly meant by his opening words in Romans 7:9: "Once I was alive apart from the law." Paul, according to Henry, by describing himself as "alive," meant only that:

> He thought himself in a very good condition, he was alive in his own opinion and apprehension, very secure and confident in the goodness of his state . . . when he was a Pharisee, for it was the common temper of that generation of men that they had a very good conceit of themselves and Paul was then like the rest of them, and the reason was he was then without the law . . . [in the sense that:] though himself a great student of the law . . . he had the letter of the law . . . but . . . not the spiritual meaning of it.[3]

Henry then parses Paul's expression "But when the commandment came, sin sprang to life and I died" as follows:

> Paul then saw . . . in sin which he had not seen before . . . [thus Paul "died" in the sense that, as Henry imagines Paul himself saying:] "I lost that good opinion which I had had of myself and came to be of another mind . . . [T]he commandment convinced me that I was in . . . a state of death because of sin."[4]

Note how determined Henry is to treat everything Paul said in Romans 7:9 as a mere figure of speech. Compulsively driven to block any attempt to take Paul's "I was alive" and his "I died" literally, Henry "spins" Paul as meaning that he was "alive" only in the sense of being bloated with exaggerated self-esteem and "dead" only in the sense of finally being humbled. Matthew Henry's allusions to Paul speaking figuratively are thus illusory.

Likewise, for Henry to describe Paul as "a great student of the law" who was simultaneously "apart from the law" as an adult is ludicrous.

Douglas J. Moo on Romans 7:9

Douglas J. Moo of Wheaton College Graduate School in Illinois concurs with Henry:

> The seemingly obvious explanation [of Romans 7:9] is that Paul is referring to an experience in his own life.

Moo then explains why the "obvious" explanation must be deemed instead as "seemingly" obvious. Please note the key assumption embedded in this quote:

> But this interpretation has a serious snag. . . . *Adam and Eve are the only human beings who ever truly passed from "life" to "death."*[5]

Dr. Moo offers no Scripture to validate this as a "serious snag," nor can he. Moo simply affirms a belief that has long been assumed *a priori* without Scripture. Nor does Moo even explain why it would be *bad* to believe that each of us, early in life, replicates Adam's and Eve's fall from life to death prior to moving back in the opposite direction via the new birth.

Would that premise somehow make us prideful? Would Adam and Eve up in heaven be miffed? I hardly think so. Moo and many theologians simply *prefer* to oppose a literal explanation of what Paul said in Romans 7:9. To help us all understand what they assume Paul meant to say, Dr. Moo explains:

> We must interpret [Paul's] key verbs [in Roman 7:9] *subjectively.* Paul "*thought* he was alive" before he understood the law; he "*came to realize* that he was dead" afterward.[6]

Moo is by no means alone. Consider another well-known Bible scholar.

F. F. Bruce on Romans 7:9

Echoing Matthew Henry and Douglas Moo, F. F. Bruce rhapsodizes Paul's "I was alive" as meaning only that "[Just as] Adam was not conscious of any sinful inclination until his obedience was tested,"[7] so also Paul was "alive" only in the sense that *he, too*, was not yet aware of being tested. Actually, Adam had no innate "sinful inclination" prior to his fall. He sinned despite a lack of such. How odd that Bruce would cite the moment Paul experienced spiritual death as nothing more than a change in mental perspective.

As for Paul's "I died," Bruce paraphrases him as saying, "Without a law to stir it into life, sin lay dormant; but when I was confronted with the law, sin sprang to life and laid me low."[8]

In other words, Bruce perceives Paul's spiritual "death" as simply a moment of ego deflation. At least Bruce agrees that Paul was not describing his own experience as unique, but as something experienced by mankind across the world. But the experience Paul was generalizing for the entire human race was much, much more significant than scholarly Dr. Bruce thinks!

Grant R. Osborne on Romans 7:9

Grant R. Osborne and others he references agree with Bruce that "Paul uses his own experience to describe the basic human situation."[9] He even expresses some doubt about the *status quo* view that Paul's statements must be interpreted figuratively rather than literally. He writes:

> There may be double meaning in *I died*, referring both to the death of [Paul's] naïve presumption that he was all right and to the spiritual death that characterizes every sinner.[10]

Kudos are due Grant Osborne! While tipping his hat to those who interpret Romans 7:9 subjectively, he senses that a literal interpretation may be what Paul intended and even lets it peek through. Still, Osborne demurs from concluding that Paul, had he died *physically* prior to his first sinful act, would thus have died *spiritually alive* and entered heaven. Just one more mind-step at that point and Grant Osborne, instead of yours truly, could have been the one urging the Church to recognize Romans 7:9 as proof that salvation is automatic prior to a moment of recognized moral culpability. Curiously, Osborne muses, "Still, one wonders when

Paul would ever have been 'without law' in a culture where the Torah was central from infancy on."[11]

Surely Dr. Osborne must know that no matter how much a child—even a Jewish child—hears and even memorizes commands from the Torah, he cannot conceive of disobedience resulting in moral culpability until he reaches a certain age, whatever that age may be.

Everett F. Harrison on Romans 7:9

Lockstep with Henry, Moo, Bruce and Osborne, Everett F. Harrison (under editing by Frank E. Gaebelein et al.)[12] urges:

> Paul's statement that he was once alive apart from the law should be taken in a relative sense, for there was no time in his life . . . when he was unrelated to the law.

Have Osborne and Harrison forgotten their own childhood? All children, including Jewish children, grow through stages of awareness prior to feeling the full impact of law. The fact that Paul spoke of a time when he was "apart from the law" despite being Jewish proves that he was speaking of his own transformation from one state to another *in early childhood*, not to a later subjective experience as an adult.

Harrison's next comment is hardly a surprise: "[Paul's] 'I died' is subjective in its force. He felt within himself the sentence of death."

Scholar after scholar thus insists that Paul was merely *feeling* spiritually alive or *feeling* spiritually dead rather than *being* spiritually alive and then *dying* spiritually. Commentaries galore keep propagating this belabored argument from silence. Thus, to a man, they run interference, blocking Paul's validation of an age of accountability and leaving us all perceiving the total number of saved people as hardly more than a tiny pittance of mankind. That is how theologians we trust have unwittingly bequeathed a tragically Pyrrhic view of God's victory over evil upon us.

Other Comments on the Fate of Children Who Die

R. Albert Mohler, Jr., president of the Southern Baptist Theological Seminary, Louisville, Kentucky, in a 2005 blog titled "In the Shadow of Death—The Little Ones Are Safe with Jesus," affirms the salvation of children who die while morally unaccountable as "biblically and theologically sustainable." Apparently unaware that he is describing a large majority of all who have ever lived in the past as saved, Mohler quotes only three proof texts to back up his assertion. Obviously, a blog is not a treatise. One text is 2 Corinthians 5:10 (which I have also quoted), a verse that leads Mohler to comment:

> The Bible clearly teaches that every person will be judged for his or her own sin, not for Adam's sin . . . [i.e., judged] for sins consciously committed during our earthly lives. . . . Have those who died in infancy committed such deeds? I believe not, for they have not yet developed the capacity to know good from evil.[13]

Yet, elsewhere in the same blog Mohler says the opposite, opining that:

> Those infants [who died in an Asian tsunami] are in heaven, but not because they were not sinners. The Bible teaches that we are all conceived in sin and born in sin, and each of us is a sinner from the moment we draw our first breath.[14]

Granting that a sinful *nature* is present, if indeed sin is an evil *act* or intent that has to be "consciously committed" or mentally indulged by someone who "knows good from evil," describing an infant as a "sinner" must mean that infants are worthy of condemnation after all. Having to keep Augustine and his doctrine of "total depravity" in one's rearview mirror at all times certainly can cause befuddlement.

Not that Mohler agrees with Augustine in every respect! Mohler adds:

> Those infants are in heaven, but not because any of them were baptized. The practice of infant baptism has led to multiple theological confusions [one of which is the fate of infants who die, hence] . . . significant Christian leaders . . . including Ambrose of Milan and Augustine of Hippo,

taught the doctrine of baptismal regeneration, [which assumes that] . . . baptized infants who die . . . go to heaven while unbaptized infants do not.[15]

Back in an era when infant mortality rates were much higher than at present, could Augustine *et al.* have been dangling infant baptism as a way of luring even unbelieving parents to join the church? If so, biblical precedent for infant baptism was hardly a matter of concern to Augustine, and standards for admittance to membership in congregations were being ominously compromised. Mohler adds:

The Bible clearly teaches the doctrine of election but it nowhere suggests that all those who die in infancy are not among the elect. Even the Westminster Confession . . . states the matter only in the positive sense, affirming that all elect infants are received into heaven. It does not require belief in the existence of any non-elect infants.[16]

Of course it does! To speak of "elect infants" is meaningless unless other infants are non-elect. If "elect infants" are received into heaven, non-elect infants who happen to die as infants are screaming in hell. Either the framers of the Westminster Confession were having momentary second thoughts or else they just could not summon the grit to admit how blatantly their Augustinian view of election misrepresents God's merciful provision for teeming populations of deceased children over ages of time.

Mohler ends by assuring us that Charles Hodge, B. B. Warfield, Charles Spurgeon and John Newton all believed very strongly in an age of accountability. That is more comforting, but how much better if we could all see Jesus and the apostle Paul at the head of Mohler's list.

In Summary

Now we see what has kept the salvation of *billions* of morally unaccountable children hidden from the Church. Scholars, over eras of time, have been blocking that important doctrine's chance to be as recognized in the Epistles as it already is in the Gospels. By opting to preserve a needless "status" for Adam and Eve and, in some minds at least, to reinforce Augustine's overstated concept called "total depravity," they have also unwittingly left God's victory over evil looking tragically Pyrrhic. The time has come for all this theological blundering to be undone and replaced.

Christians have been left long enough with no choice but to mutter incoherently about the possible destiny of literally *billions* of wee children. We have also been forced to ponder our God as improbably unable to win anything but a Pyrrhic victory over evil in the ongoing contest of the ages.

What Paul strongly implies in all of the above passages from his Epistles is also something Isaiah 57:1 chidingly describes as a sovereign, albeit "undercover," operation our merciful God has long been sustaining.

Listen! We Are Being *Chided* by God!

Chiding, as opposed to a stinging rebuke, is something God applies to us via Isaiah. Why? Because of our failure to recognize unusually high numbers of early deaths as a hint that God's mercy is subtly at work behind the scenes of earth. Isaiah wrote:

> The righteous perish, and no one ponders it in his heart; devout men are taken away, and no one understands that the righteous are taken away to be spared from *ra'* [a Hebrew word for "disaster"] (Isaiah 57:1).

Because early death during most of mankind's tenure on earth has always been preponderantly the early death of *children*, a comment on Isaiah 57:1 is merited in any discussion about the age of accountability.

Apparently, God is bemused by how oblivious we are to a category of choices he alone sovereignly controls. I refer to the regrettable but often needed option God alone possesses to ordain early death, not as a punishment but as a mercy guided by divine foreknowledge.

Of course we all desire length of days on earth for ourselves and for all whom we love. That is also what God prefers to grant us. Still, on occasion, God in his wisdom ordains a seemingly premature but actually benign exit from this world so as to shield someone he loves from encountering what in Hebrew is called *ra'*.

Depending on the context, *ra'* in Hebrew can mean either "disaster" or "moral evil." For example, in Jeremiah 29:11, *ra'* is translated as "harm."[17]

New International Version translators—apparently thinking that God cuts lives short to keep devout people from yielding to temptation later in life—end Isaiah 57:1 with *ra'* translated as "evil." I object that navigating a gauntlet of temptation is appointed to everyone who lives long enough to discern good from evil. Overcoming temptation by the grace of God is what most enables us to glorify God in Job-like ways.

We may also ask, would a just God intervene to keep some people from succumbing to temptation and then judge others who would not have sinned had he done the same for them?

For reasons such as these, I propose that *ra'*, a key Hebrew word in Isaiah 57:1, should be translated as "disaster" or "calamity," not "evil." To understand why, imagine God not only foreseeing but also solving a crisis awaiting a man named Bill as follows:

1. God foresees Bill repenting and being saved as an adult only if a friend named Joe proclaims the gospel to Bill at a crucial moment in Bill's life. Not only that, but Joe is the only messenger Bill will respect enough to heed.

2. God also foresees that Bill would be lost forever because Joe will fail by not being on time with the message.

3. However, repentance foreknown by God is as valid to God as repentance in real time, à la Romans 4:17 ("God ... calls things that are not as though they were"). Thus, God, foreseeing Bill's potential repentance, spares Bill from suffering eternal *ra'* due to Joe's future failure by causing Bill to die prior to his Romans 7:9 "death."

   Joe's foreseen failure thus costs God the service Bill would have rendered as a believer and costs Bill the privilege of serving God as a believer. Joe loses a greater opportunity because Bill will not be there! Joe's foreseen failure does not, however, condemn Bill to eternal suffering. Note also that God does not violate Joe's free will by forcing him to minister to Bill.

Conversely, if God foresees that Bill's final choice in life will be irreconcilably evil impenitence, God does not take Bill as a baby. Instead, God lets Bill live out his life on earth if only to procreate so that some of Bill's descendants may experience the salvation Bill the progenitor scorned. Virtually everyone welcomed into heaven is descended from others who reject the privilege. Merely by procreating, God-rejecters may end up serving God anyway, albeit unwittingly, simply by fostering descendants who will enjoy His kingdom without them.

Some will respond, "If people I do not lead to Christ will reach heaven anyway because God, foreknowing my failure, has already taken them as babies, why should I bother trying to lead anyone to faith?"

The best response to that objection is this: *Those who dismiss God's greater glory and other people's greater privilege in life as insufficient motivation to share the gospel are not messengers God wants to use anyway. They also forfeit incredibly greater degrees of joy for themselves in heaven.*

Crossing a New Threshold

What more must I say? I appeal both to theologians who honor the Bible as the Word of God as well as to rank-and-file Christians everywhere to speak out in favor of the age of accountability as found in Paul's teachings. Let us grant the apostle his right, after all these centuries of misconstruing part of his message, to have all his Romans 7:9-related teachings received *literally* at last!

After centuries of misreading Paul's crucially literal mini-autobiography in Romans 7:9, and its vital link with his many other related texts—some of them from three other Epistles—will responsible Christian authors take care to amend texts published in the past as needed? At least may friends of biblical truth everywhere affirm salvation as a "given" for every fetus/baby/child who dies prior to a moment of accountability.

If only someone had corrected the above serious misreading of Paul's message much earlier, perhaps gifted pastor Rob Bell would not have felt harried into urging a million or more mostly young Christian readers of his book *Love Wins* to credit salvation as universal. Moreover, if the theological community refuses to accept the correction treatised here, predictably we will have more Rob Bells dispensing wrong solutions to valid intuitions in days to come.

Accrediting this vital tenet also inspires us to praise God for sovereignly exploiting early death as a means of mercy for the billions of children whose response to the gospel he foresaw as real but for our delinquency as God's messengers. By that foresight God has guaranteed that his kingdom will indeed embrace a *majority* of those for whom Jesus shed his atoning blood and rose from the dead.

Do all who have died *in utero*, at birth and during, shall we say, the first five or six years of life, really comprise a majority of mankind? Assuredly, yes! My next chapter, aided by estimates from the archive of medical science, places that number at close to 70 percent of all who have ever been conceived in the womb.

Along with hosts of holy angels and the billions our Lord is in the process of redeeming from this sinful world, we can celebrate not only our God's *moral* victory over evil but also his genuinely *numerical* triumph as well. Now we know why Jesus could say jubilantly, as recorded in three Gospels, "Let the little children come to me . . . *for the kingdom of God belongs to such as these.*"

It May Actually *Help* Our Witness
If We Are Perceived as a Majority

I sense that many unbelieving people subliminally spurn Christianity because they perceive it as accepted by only a minority of mankind. They want to be *in* with the really big crowd.

Well, then, let us now invite unbelievers everywhere, saying, "Come join the *majority* of mankind for eternity!" The vastness of the cosmos awaits our combined witness to the triumph of God's grace over evil, both morally and numerically, in this once-and-for-all-time planetary arena called Earth.

Having confirmed the "age of accountability" as validly biblical, let us now examine historical evidence confirming that a large majority of mankind has been spared from otherwise inevitable judgment by dying under the cover of this merciful shield afforded by an age of accountability.

MEASURING INFANT MORTALITY

Citizens in medically advanced modern nations tend not to know that most of mankind, over the ages, has died early in life if not in the womb or at birth. Typically, low infant and child mortality rates prevailing in developed regions are still not all that common in the rest of the world even today. Surveys indicate that consistently high child mortality rates have prevailed historically.

Apart from diseases more commonly fatal to the elderly—cancer, heart failure, stroke, diabetes and dementia—epidemics of cholera, bubonic plague, influenza, smallpox, meningitis, typhoid, dysentery, scarlet fever, malaria, pneumonia, typhus and whooping cough, plus malnutrition, war, accidents and natural disasters have preponderantly scourged the very young. Virtually everyone who reached puberty or adulthood throughout most of mankind's tenure on earth did so by surviving one or more serious diseases or a near-tragedy. The majority of children perished.

One aspect of medical science I have personally observed and learned to appreciate is the priority it tends to assign to recordkeeping. My now-deceased first wife, Carol Joy, during the 15 years we served as missionaries in a remote—and at that time not even governed—part of what is now Papua (the western half of a huge island known as New Guinea), served dozens of isolated lowland villages as a registered nurse.

Our Personal Encounter with Shocking Death Rates

The government in what was then Netherlands New Guinea supplied Carol with quantities of medicine on condition that she keep and submit records on how the medicine was used for how many patients afflicted by which diseases. Our adventures there are narrated in my first book, *Peace Child*.

Treating on average 800 patients per month out of a clinic I built for her, Carol began saving lives. In one month marked by a severe epidemic, Carol administered 2,600 treatments. During epidemics of influenza, whooping cough and mumps, there is no doubt she often saved several lives a day. Overall, I estimate that Carol probably saved an average of one life per day during the years we resided in the remote malarial lowlands of New Guinea.

At one point, Carol decided to do research on child mortality by interviewing tribal women. Fluent in the tribal language by 1969, she asked mothers in two nearby villages the same two questions: (1) How many times have you been pregnant? (2) How many of the children birthed were stillborn or subsequently died as children?

Their responses indicated a 60 percent child death rate. Three other factors, however, signified a death rate that was even higher prior to our arrival:

1. Carol herself had recovered some of their surviving children from deadly diseases in the seven years that had elapsed since our arrival. Apart from her ministration, some of these children also would have been among the dead. Plus, both of us, by arranging to vaccinate some 2,000 tribal people against an approaching cholera epidemic, had kept that severe menace from entering these same villages.

2. Few of the women Carol interviewed would have recognized early miscarriages as failed pregnancies. They had no calendars or other means to determine if a menstrual period was overdue.

3. My success in interrupting many arrow and spear battles that otherwise would have raged out of control probably spared the lives of still more children.

We heard of a similar survey done by colleagues working among Papua's mountain tribes, yielding similar results. Each of these linguistically unique Papuan tribes had existed long enough to attain a population of at least a few hundred thousand per tribe, yet a majority of Papuan tribes at that time numbered only a few thousand people, or even less than one thousand. High child mortality rates prevailing over ages of time assuredly were the main reason populations remained so minuscule.

Papua's prenatal and first-five-years-of-life mortality rates, taken together, probably averaged 70 percent prior to the arrival of outsiders able to offer at least basic medical service.

Compare this estimate with the report in Figure 1 from the United Nations and the *CIA: The World Factbook*. The full report covers the 100 highest first-year-of-life child death rates found anywhere on earth from 1950 to 1955. From that report I quote only the top 10, all of which averaged a 25.0 percent death rate per year per nation for death in *just the first year of life only*. This of course omits pre-birth loss of life due to miscarriage, stillbirth or abortion. It also disregards the fact that many children who lived more than one year failed to reach age five. Indeed, most such surveys monitor child death, not from conception, but only from birth until, in many cases, five years of age. Thus, fetuses lost due to miscarriage and/or abortion are not included. This factor, though it raises the child mortality percentages even higher than 65 percent, tends to be ignored by medical surveys.

Surely miscarriages and abortions are more difficult to monitor. Perhaps some medical researchers disregard pre-birth child death because they do not accept the Christian belief that fetuses are already truly human.

Prior to the rise of medical expertise and increasing sanitation over the last two centuries, the figures, quoted in Figure 1, doubtless can be doubled for the world at large over previous ages.

Medical researchers generally divide statistics on child mortality into four main categories, commonly labeled as follows: *miscarriage* (indicating loss of a baby before the twentieth week of pregnancy); *stillbirth* (indicating death of a baby from the twenty-eighth week of gestation up to full-term birth); *infant mortality* (indicating death during the first year after birth); and *child mortality* (indicating death between age one and age five). With the 10 highest 1950 to 1955 first-year-of-life death rates reporting at 25 percent, as listed above, other numbers representing miscarriages, stillbirths and the mortality of children after the age of one and up to five years have yet to be added.

Figure 1

First-year-of-life death rates as a percent of live births in the 10 "most-medically challenged" nations, from 1950 to 1955[1]

1.	Burkina Faso:	30.8%
2.	Afghanistan:	27.5%
3.	East Timor:	26.4%
4.	Iran:	26.2%
5.	Sierra Leone:	24.2%
6.	Haiti:	24.2%
7.	Maldives:	23.3%
8.	Angola:	23.0%
9.	Liberia:	22.4%
10.	Gambia:	22.1%
	Average:	25.0%

Though figures for miscarriage in developing countries are rarely available, because women in developing countries rarely report them to medical researchers, the following reports from developed nations indicates rates as follows:

Thirty-one percent of all conceptions end in miscarriage, usually in the early months of pregnancy and often before women even know they are pregnant. . . . But most of the women who have miscarriages are normally fertile and subsequently become pregnant again and have babies, the study reported.

While experts have long known that miscarriages early in pregnancy are common, estimates of the rate have varied widely. The new study, using a urine test, provides the most precise data yet.[2]

Lead researcher for the above study, Dr. Allen J. Wilcox of the NIEHS (National Institute of Environmental Health Sciences) in

Research Triangle Park, North Carolina, said that even the extremely sensitive measurement technique employed "*underestimates the miscarriage rate by an unknown amount* [emphasis added] since some embryos are so defective that they never make human chorionic gonadotropin and are miscarried within days of fertilization."[3]

Another report puts the percentage of pregnancies that miscarry much higher than those specified in the above article:

> According to the March of Dimes, *as many as 50% of all pregnancies end in miscarriage* [emphasis added]—most often before a woman misses a menstrual period or even knows she is pregnant. About 15% of *recognized* pregnancies will end in a miscarriage.[4]

Pegging an estimate of miscarried pregnancies plus stillbirths, over centuries of time, at a very conservative *40 percent* (midway between the above 31 percent and 50 percent rates for developed countries), I amend the figures further as follows: I add another *25 percent* based on the 1950 to 1955 death rates for children in just the first year of life, as in Figure 1. It is likely the percentage was even higher for pre-1950 death rates, going back centuries or millennia in history, given that medical science was less advanced, and record keeping—if done at all—less sophisticated in earlier times.

Adding also another very conservative *15 percent* death rate for children who died after the first year up to the fifth year, we arrive at the following estimate for mankind's total *fetus + infant + child death rate* over ages of time:

Figure 2

Miscarriages/stillbirth:	40% very conservatively
First-year-of-life death rate:	25% likely higher
Year 1 to age 5 death rate:	15% likely higher
Overall Average, at least:	70-80%

This Figure 2 average, extended back over time to human populations existing virtually everywhere over elapsed millennia, verifies that heaven has by no means been settling for a merely Pyrrhic victory over evil. With that many children safe in our Lord's presence, *heaven was winning* even before God began adding hundreds of millions of people who have effectively prayed to be saved.

And now, as heaven's victory gains momentum with ever more survivors of child death coming to faith in Jesus Christ than in ages past, surely we have already lifted the conservative 70 percent shown in Figure 2 to a level much closer to the 80 percentile range or even higher.

It Could Hardly Be a Coincidence

In this connection, let me ask: What has contributed to the rapid increase of human population over these last two centuries? In a recent televised documentary titled *Prophets of Doom,* six authorities from as many fields of research described an amalgam of predicaments facing mankind. In one part of the discussion the panel credited humanity's last two centuries of accelerated population growth as due mainly to increasing supplies of food via mechanization. But that is only part of the story.

Having enough to eat does not guarantee a significant increase in numbers if deadly diseases still stalk the population. Yet no one on that prestigious panel mentioned that it was not until approximately two centuries ago that mankind detected dangerous microbes as a major cause of disease. Not until then did researchers also discover that— in addition to hygiene—boiling water, inoculations, vaccinations, medicines, drugs and chemicals can be applied to counter the spread of disease. Such benefits surely must not be taken for granted. These initial breakthroughs and subsequent advances came during the same decades that the Church of our Lord began to revive its zeal for missions—an until-then largely forgotten obligation!

Thousands of churches recommitted themselves to world evangelization after being awakened by the example of the Moravians, who went to many nations; William Carey, who went to India; and Robert Morrison, a British missionary trailblazer in China.

Of course the tens of thousands of pioneers who soon ventured out to master scores of languages in dozens of nations took more than the gospel with them. They also dispensed medicines and medical knowledge. They promoted peace, provided sanitary conditions for childbirth, and taught personal hygiene and healthier dietary habits.

It can hardly be coincidental that the rapid spread of the gospel across the earth was accompanied by increased efficiency in reducing child mortality rates, which until then had remained astronomically high. *Sparing children the Isaiah 57:1/Romans 7:9 way is by no means God's preference!*

It was largely to compensate for the church's truancy that God has spared billions from *ra'*, the ultimate disaster, via the otherwise unneeded Isaiah 57:1 "fail-safe." May we as God's servants continue to spread the gospel so effectively that the number of people who have to be saved "the fail-safe way" will be greatly reduced.

Salvation via early death, though it saves the soul, denies God the greater glory and denies little children the much greater privilege of living to receive the gospel and manifest God's goodness while completing their lives on this earth—presumably the only and final "arena world" in the entire cosmos.

Granted, then, that the Bible acknowledges that all who die as children are saved and that mankind's consistently high child mortality rates portend 70 percent of mankind [that is, 70 percent of everyone ever conceived in the womb] as already in heaven via that provision, what else? Let us now try to estimate the percentage of people who, surviving early death, have been saved or are yet to be saved by responding with repentance and faith to divine revelation—of which there are two categories!

6

THE TWO CATEGORIES OF DIVINE REVELATION

hristians commonly divide the entirety of what God has revealed into two major categories: *general revelation* (the "single poignancy" persuasion described earlier) and *special revelation,* which, when clearly understood and perceived in concert with general revelation, draws mankind to God with a "double poignancy" persuasion.

General revelation includes all that can be known about creation—God's artistry—along with everything that can be known via creation about the Artisan of creation, *God.*

Special revelation, conversely, includes all that God explains about himself and the plan of redemption and has sovereignly ordained to be included and preserved in the inspired canon of Old and New Testament Scripture.

Concerning these two categories of revelation, there are three competing schools of Christian thought. The first school of thought has zero support in Scripture. The second school of thought has extensive support in Scripture. Only the third school of thought, I contend, can claim total support in Scripture.

First among these three schools of thought is Universalism.

Universalism

Proponents of universalism accord God total statistical victory over evil at the cost of his own moral defeat. Everyone—usually including Satan and every demon—enters heaven eventually despite refusing to repudiate evil within a fitting period of grace. Failing to elicit repentance by persuasion, God surrenders and betrays his own infinite holiness by dispensing mercy unlawfully.

Universalists, of course, have no way to guarantee that merely entering heaven will be enough to transform brutal evildoers into noble citizens, in which case heaven may not remain heavenly for very long; but so what, as long as everyone is pain-free!

Universalism has zero support in the Bible.

Exclusivism

Most of what Exclusivism—the second school of thought—believes is indeed strongly supported by Scripture. If it were not for a few serious Exclusivist oversights, an up-and-coming third school of thought—*Inclusivism*, explained later—would not be needed at all.

In stark contrast to Universalism, proponents of Exclusivism accord God a total moral victory over evil but at the cost of a statistically Pyrrhic disaster in terms of the number of people who will be saved. Of course, Exclusivists, as in my earlier quote from Mark Galli, think that an enormous defeat in terms of numbers is of no major concern to God, nor should it be to us.

Let me explain how Exclusivists, despite quoting and applying a number of Scriptures correctly, infer ultimately that God's obvious moral victory over evil will end up tragically Pyrrhic. First of all, many Exclusivists accept Augustine's view of humanity as totally incapable of responding to either category of revelation (a doctrine known as "total depravity") apart from a special infusion of grace, which is given only to "the elect." Many agree with both Augustine and John Calvin that God is interested only in people he elects to be saved, and it makes no difference to him whether they are a majority or a minority of mankind. Even Christ's atonement avails only for the elect.

That said, all Exclusivists—Reformed or otherwise—value God's general revelation as informative only. Special revelation, conversely, is both informative *and salvific!* "Salvific" means viably appointed to induce genuine repentance and faith in the minds, hearts and wills of otherwise indifferent people. Due to their definition of general revelation as informative only, Exclusivists—in terms of who will be saved—focus "exclusively" on special revelation's salvific ingathering of two "remnants" of people amid the masses of mankind.

One remnant consists of those who, anticipating a Savior promised by special revelation's Old Testament prophets, found eternal life. One Old Testament prophet, Jeremiah, described in his writings all this with one grand comment:

> Israel was holy to the LORD, the *firstfruits* of [God's] harvest (Jeremiah 2:3).

The second "remnant" is what Jeremiah designated as the "harvest" that ensues after the first fruits have been gathered. The harvest, of course, entails the larger number of people subsequently saved by the virtually worldwide proclamation of Jesus as special revelation's long-before promised Messiah/Savior.

I find that many Evangelicals influenced by Exclusivism, if asked for an estimate of how many people may be saved, tend to regard both of the above two "remnants" combined as totaling no more than 5 to 10 percent of mankind. If, in fact, that is how God's plan for the ages culminates, God is indeed content with a merely Pyrrhic victory over evil.

To be sure, Exclusivists genuinely believe that the Bible backs their Pyrrhic premises. I know, because I began my own Christian ministry as an Exclusivist, believing there was no other scripturally support-able alternative to Universalism (which I knew to be unbiblical).

In a later chapter, I review the main texts that Exclusivists quote to support their view of general revelation as informative only. I will also show how, generations ago, Exclusivism's primary founders—by loading certain texts on one side of a theological fulcrum and leaving others on the grass—bequeathed a "tilted" soteriology to the church of Jesus Christ.

Later generations, perhaps more focused on Exclusivist com-mentaries on Scripture than on Scripture itself, dutifully continue downgrading general revelation's immortal significance as a result.

Until recently, a large majority of Exclusivists thought anyone who was not an Exclusivist had to be a Universalist. What other option could there be? My premise in *Heaven Wins,* that a third school of thought—*Inclusivism*—is biblically authentic without snitching a single thread from Universalism, will be a shock to many Exclusivists.

Let me now introduce that third option.

Inclusivism

Whereas Exclusivists regard general revelation as informative only and special revelation as both informative and salvific, Inclusivists, by contrast, regard general revelation as both informative and salvific and special revelation as *even more deeply informative* and *even more effectively and widely salvific!*

Now you understand, if you didn't before, the primary difference between Exclusivism—ensconced everywhere in Evangelical churches, seminaries and even missionary societies—and its vibrantly reassertive (hopefully even resurgent) competitor, Inclusivism!

I myself, a former Exclusivist, felt so alone when both the weight of Scripture and mission field experience made me an Inclusivist. In the on-and-off struggle between these two competing schools of Christian thought, Exclusivists have long been claiming the higher ground. I think that is about to change. Inclusivism has languished for so long, needing a champion or two who can stent theology's circulatory system and unclog the thrombosis that blocks the "Body" from granting Inclusivism its long-overdue recognition.

Well, I've been through pre-op; I'm scrubbed and ready, lancet in hand. But—thank God—I am not as alone as I thought. At least three conservative theologians—Millard Erickson, William Crockett and James Sigountos—and several seasoned senior missionaries have begun publishing Inclusivist books and papers. But first I must explain a problem Exclusivists and Inclusivists share, not as to what they teach, but as to something they both tend to overlook.

A Major Historical/Biblical Oversight

Exclusivists and Inclusivists both either do not know or prefer to ignore the significance of the very high child mortality rates documented in my previous chapter. The fact that medical surveys (which I cite in chapter 5) find at least 70 percent of humanity perishing in the womb or in childhood, hence entering heaven, is fraught with profound implications for theology as a whole.

This insight tends to jar Exclusivists simply because their theology has for so long inured them to the premise that only a relatively small number of "elect" people will be saved. Inclusivists, however, by accrediting general revelation as salvific for at least a few in every age worldwide, are much more accustomed to thinking of higher percentages of people being saved than their Exclusivist compadres. That is why I think Inclusivists will be delighted to discover that adding the percentages of people saved by both special and general revelation to the 80 percent or more secured by child mortality lifts estimates of how many people will be saved substantially higher, perhaps even beyond 85 percent!

Finally, Inclusivists have another problem: They tend not to know more than two or three Bible texts related to general revelation. My next two chapters offer a much wider abundance of texts.

7

GENERAL REVELATION— IS IT INFORMATIVE ONLY?

Passages in the Bible that evince creation as attesting to the person of God are deemed as acknowledging what is commonly called "general revelation." These passages divide into two categories: (A) those attesting general revelation as informative about God without specifying whether the information bestowed can be salvific or not, and (B) passages that attest general revelation as informative for everyone but also potentially salvific for at least a minority of mankind.

We begin by reviewing seven passages that fit the first category—passages that Exclusivists are most likely to quote. Then a second category with 15 passages will be added, those that honor general revelation as more than merely informative—passages that aver its age-long salvific potential. Some of these are passages that not only many Exclusivists but also many Inclusivists do not even know are in the Bible.

Category "A" Texts: General Revelation as Informative

David and Solomon's Perspective

By far the most oft-quoted "flagship" text on the topic of general revelation is King David's grand depiction of the heavens and the earth as a cosmos-wide media network in the hand of God. In Psalm 19, David declared:

> The heavens declare the glory of God; the skies proclaim the work of his hands. Day after day they pour forth speech;

night after night they display knowledge. There is no speech or language where their voice is not heard. Their voice goes out into all the earth, their words to the ends of the world (Psalm 19:1-4).

Though these four verses do not state that lost people find salvation due to the evocative testimony of creation, later I will show that one of the apostles quotes part of the Psalm 19 verses to that effect. Psalm 97:6 echoes David's eloquence with:

The heavens proclaim his righteousness . . . all the peoples see his glory.

Along with his father, David, Solomon is another Old Testament notable with a keen appreciation for general revelation: "[God] has made everything beautiful in its time" (Ecclesiastes 3:11). Yes! Sunrise, lovely at 6:00 AM, would be extremely discomfiting if suddenly it popped up at midnight. Childlike behavior, adorable in a 3-year-old, is entirely out of place in a 33-year-old. Solomon continued in verse 11:

[God] has also set eternity in the hearts of men; yet they cannot fathom what God has done from beginning to end.

Solomon seems to be describing people who, like Job, already know God but also want to know more about him. Just as Job had no inkling that his response to God amid suffering bore immense significance for angelic observers across the cosmos, so too all who find God via general revelation possess limited awareness. General revelation, at a minimum, imparts enough knowledge of God to reveal him as an object of saving faith and a source of guidance for someone who supplicates him for mercy, but not enough to facilitate a deep grasp of God's long-term plans unfolding in history.

Paul's Perspective in Acts and the Epistles

Paul and Barnabas, experiencing a close encounter of a cross-cultural kind in a pagan city called Lystra, appealed to the witness of general revelation to help resolve a pagan audience's serious misinterpretation of the apostles' mission.

Learning that they were being mistaken for two pagan gods—Zeus and Hermes—Paul and Barnabas rushed out into the crowd, tearing their clothes in protest and shouting:

> Men, why are you doing this? We too are only men, human like you. We are bringing you good news, telling you to turn from these worthless things to the living God [known to the Greeks as *Theos*] (Acts 14:15-17).

Pagans in Lystra worshiped Zeus, a god perceived as ruling over other deities—Apollo, Artemis, Ares, Hermes, to name a few. Pagan Greek-speaking people also knew, however, that some of their own philosophers, pondering the natural order of the cosmos (general revelation), had inferred the existence of a deity far greater than Zeus.

Such a being could not fairly be designated in the same way as their other gods—that is, any god with a small "g" or any deity with a small "d." No, a deity above the king of their gods became known as *Theos* with a capital "T" as it were, in the special sense of *the* Theos.

Zeus, whom pagans regarded as the offspring of two other deities—Kronos and Rhea—obviously could not hold a candle next to Theos, the God who was gradually gaining renown among various philosophers as the Creator of all things, who is himself uncreated. This Theos was the "uncaused Cause," the "unmoved Mover."

It was mainly on the basis of that definition of the term, derived from the influence of general revelation, that the term *Theos* gained recognition, first in the Septuagint and later in the New Testament, as a valid Greek a.k.a—an "also known as" —for *Elohim*!

If that helpful lexical matchup had been rejected by the translators of the Septuagint before Christ and, subsequently, by the apostles after him (if they had spurned "Theos" as "too pagan"), the word "theology" would not be in common use in English today. We would probably be referring to "elohimology" instead.

Likewise, if *Deus*—a Latin equivalent for *Theos*—had been rejected apostolically, we today would likely not be saying "deity" but "elohimity."

Thus it transpired in Lystra that Paul and Barnabas—shelving special revelation-generated names for God, such as *Elohim*, *Adonai* and *Yahweh*—proclaimed *Theos* as the One who, in the past, had "let all nations go their own way" (Acts 14:16).

When the pagan unbelievers, mentioned earlier, wrong-headedly insisted on going their own way down through the ages, *Theos* let them. He also let them reap a wide variety of consequences. But Paul and Barnabas immediately balanced Acts 14:16 with this very positive declaration in v. 17:

> Yet he [*Theos*] has not left himself without testimony: He has shown kindness by giving you rain from heaven and crops in their seasons; he provides you with plenty of food and fills your hearts with joy.

When Paul and Barnabas preached in Jewish synagogues, special revelation needed little, if any, introduction. Among pagans such as Lycaonians in Lystra, appealing to general revelation became the apostles' logical segue to special revelation.

Another frequently quoted reference on general revelation beckons from the book of Romans. The apostle Paul, trained as a Jewish rabbi, perhaps had Psalm 19:1-4 and maybe Psalm 97:6 in mind when he penned the following immortal words:

> For since the creation of the world God's invisible qualities— his eternal power and divine nature—have been clearly seen, being understood from what has been made, so that men are without excuse (Romans 1:20).

In some Exclusivist-leaning commentaries and sermons, Paul's "clearly seen" and "being understood" in Romans 1:20 end up sounding more like "dimly sensed" and "barely perceived." Nevertheless, it is true that Paul, in Romans 1:20, does not specify general revelation as salvific or not salvific, but merely informative. Further along in Romans, Paul credits general revelation as etching requirements of God's law in unexpected places:

When Gentiles, who do not have the law, do by nature things required by the law, they are a law for themselves, even though they do not have the law, since they show that the requirements of the law are written on their hearts, their consciences also bearing witness, and their thoughts now accusing, now even defending them (Romans 2:14-15).

Again, Paul does not specify general revelation as salvific or not salvific but only as very informative. Assuredly, pre-Christian Hawaiians paralleled Old Testament law by dedicating cities of refuge for fugitives. Even the stone-age Yali tribesmen of whom I wrote in *Lords of the Earth* honored places of refuge, a corollary to cities of refuge provided for God's people in the Old Testament (see Numbers 35).

In my book *Eternity in Their Hearts*, I document Dyak headhunters in Kalimantan, Indonesia, sending their "sins" floating away on a "scapeboat" reminiscent of Judaism's scapegoat (see Leviticus 16:6-10,20-22).

And these are just a few examples. Surely, practices such as these are not things the Evil One would want to imprint on human societies. Surely, practices such as these are by-products of God's general revelation. May *he* get the credit for doing just what Paul said—writing such things on the hearts of Gentiles!

Paul does not limit Christians to Scripture as their sole source for truth. General revelation's expansive fields of truth are theirs to explore as well. Hence, Paul counseled:

Finally, brothers, whatever is true, whatever is noble, whatever is right, whatever is pure, whatever is lovely, whatever is admirable—if anything is excellent or praiseworthy—think about such things (Philippians 4:8).

Paul's delightful list of ponderable "whatevers" covers all that can be mined from both categories of revelation.

Finally, note also how succinctly John's Gospel identifies Jesus our Lord as sourcing both general and special revelation:

The true light that gives light to every man was coming into the world (John 1:9).

Thus, the same Source that always grants a general illumination to everyone everywhere still was coming into our world to shine upon as many people as possible in new and very special ways.

Granted, the above seven texts do not specify general revelation as salvific, but neither do they affirm it as non-salvific. They simply affirm that general revelation exists to God's glory and for mankind's insight. It is precisely at this point that Exclusivists illogically assume that because the above seven texts do not specify general revelation as salvific, that alone is sufficient proof—arguing from silence—that it is not salvific. Case closed. Further examination of the Bible on the subject is pointless.

The case is *not* closed! In my next chapter, I showcase with great delight an array of 15 grievously overlooked Old and New Testament texts in which Gentiles far removed from both Israel and the Church are described as God's people. Because they were saved apart from special revelation, we have no choice but to recognize Christ as saving such on the basis of their faith response to general revelation. In the light of the witness of these 15 verses, the silence of the above 7 texts as to general revelation's capacity to save was due to the fact that prior to Augustine, God's ability to save a remnant of Gentiles via general revelation was so widely accepted as a given that it hardly needed to be stated.

8

GENERAL REVELATION— SALVIFIC FOR AT LEAST A FEW!

Category "B" Texts: General Revelation Is Salvific

1. The Book of Job

The book of Job, believed by many to predate the actual writing of Genesis, appears to have been added to the canon of Scripture primarily to celebrate general revelation's potentially salvific presence everywhere. Defining general revelation as salvific does not portend that it brings everyone or even a majority of mankind to salvation. The gospel of special revelation evokes much more measurable response—beginning, of course, with people already brought into relationship with God by general revelation.

The main difference is that the witness of general revelation is just simply and totally always there!

The book of Job is packed with references to God intermingled with scores of references to details of creation cited as bases for instruction and knowledge of him. Yet, Job contains no mention of God establishing a covenant with mankind; no mention of Scripture; no mention of sacred feasts; no mention of a temple or a priesthood; no mention of an encoded list of commandments.

The only covenant in the book of Job is one Job himself initiated:

I made a covenant with my eyes not to look lustfully at a girl (31:1).

Indeed, the apostle Paul, ages later, when he wrote of Gentiles having elements of divine law "written on their hearts" (Romans 2:14-15), may have had Job and friends in mind.

Many Christians assume no one even knows for sure where Job's homeland—Uz—was. Others think the book of Job originated far to the east of Palestine in what is now lofty Uzbekistan with its colder climate. As one might expect, Job mentions ice, frost, snow and hail more times than any other book in the Bible. Not only so, but the very name—Uzbekistan—joins three words. *Uz* is the name of a place; *bek* signifies a noble person and *–istan* means "encampment." Hence, *Uzbekistan* means "the place where the noble one of Uz encamps" (or, "the camp of the great one of Uz").

Job and his friends, despite having no inspired Scripture to teach them about God, were hardly stymied in faraway Uz. They acclaimed "God above" or "the God of heaven" as the one "who teaches more to us than to the beasts of the earth" (Job 35:11). As a result, Job knew how to worship (see 1:20). He and his people offered sacrifice to atone for sin (see 1:5). They spurned idolatry (see 12:6). Job, at least, was monogamous (see 2:9 and 31:1).

Job and his fellow Uzians pondered not only ice, frost, snow, hail and rain but also constellations of stars like Orion and the Pleiades, tempests, thunder, lightning and calamities like floods, droughts, sickness and war. They observed the ways of donkeys, spiders, snakes, moths, ostriches, hawks, eagles and wild donkeys—all the while seeking to fathom why God does not consistently ordain prosperity for righteous folk versus disaster for evildoers. They were ever seeking more and fresher knowledge of the One they knew not as Elohim but as the "God of heaven."

The key insights Job and his friends derived via general revelation were not nearly as conclusive as we, blessed with special revelation from God millennia later, understand and enjoy. Still, keenly aware of what pleases versus what displeases their Creator, Job and his friends appear to have lived well above the ethical standards of many folk in more illumined modern societies.

I submit that the book of Job attests that general revelation is both informative and salvific. What Job and his friends observed in their environment illumined their minds and gripped their consciences sufficient to cause them to cast themselves on the mercy of "the God of heaven" and live in relationship with him. Pondering these astute Uzians, eavesdropping on their conversations, prepares us to expect that the Bible will surely reference people such as them elsewhere. As we will see, it does.

The "Jobs" (and "Jobesses"!) whom God has been harvesting via general revelation over ages of time are but a small, partially instructed corpus of believers. Even so, the mere fact that they exist at all as "people of peace" in virtually every village in every age establishes them as a significant minority among the redeemed.

Like Job, they suffer chaos generated by heedless pagan neighbors. Also like Job, as "people of peace," they temper that chaos, even if marginally.

Jobs as "First Responders"

Little do Jobs scattered throughout the pagan world know that their Creator has a hidden calling reserved for them—a calling most Jobs and Jobesses never get to fulfill. All across the world, God's Jobs and Jobesses are ideally prepared to serve, however unwittingly, as "first responders" to biblical revelation, should it ever be conveyed to them by faithful messengers. Biblical revelation, a much more multifaceted message entrusted to worshipers elsewhere, is meant initially to edify Job-like first responders, thus enabling them to bring their harder-to-persuade pagan neighbors to faith.

Job-like first responders already know the language and culture a foreign missionary must learn. Teach biblical revelation to a Job and he will teach it to others. I described several such in my first three books: *Peace Child, Lords of the Earth,* and *Eternity in Their Hearts.* But Exclusivist influence in that season of my life restrained me from identifying them correctly as Job-like first responders.

I think it goes almost without saying that due to the Church's historically customary practice of warehousing the gospel within limited perimeters, a majority of Job-like people never got to enjoy the privilege of serving as first responders. Messengers who refused to take the gospel out into the world, fearing the task of communicating it as too difficult, have had no concept of how readily their mission could have been facilitated with Job-ian aid.

As for the many non-Jobs whom Jobs equipped with the gospel could have helped bring to faith, assumedly God had to take them as children, à la Isaiah 57:1, so as not to lose them forever.

Because of messenger delinquency, Job-like persons, churches that could have supported delinquent messengers and potentially repentant non-Jobs who otherwise would have survived early death and believed miss out! Most important, delinquent messengers deny God the greater honor he merits by saving people as responders to truth (who then become His servants) rather than as children taken while still securely covered by the sacrifice of Christ.

Exclusivists commonly warn as follows: Telling Christians that some people in pagan domains find redemption via general revelation will seriously curtail missionary motivation to proclaim special revelation. Rather than say, "Here I am, Lord; send me!" Christians will respond with, "Fine! Let God save them that way; I have other things to do."

Really?

Why would presenting general revelation as salvific for a few diminish urgency to spread the gospel for the many? If a few people escape from a burning building before the firemen arrive, does that discourage the firemen from rescuing others who are still trapped? Not at all! Would a fireman say, "If we can't save all the people who were in danger, we'll shut off the alarm and stay in our beds"? No, firemen appreciate any help those who are already safe can give to complete the rescue of others. And those found to be already safe from the fire may also need help to find "new lodging"!

Whether acting to save some or all, rescuers rescue!

The Exclusivist objection that crediting general revelation as salvific for a few undermines motivation to save the many is simply ill-conceived.

How ironic! By failing to teach that God has prepared linguistically and culturally adept Job-like persons who are ready to help as first responders, Exclusivism actually tends to turn some Christians away from missionary service simply by making the task of converting pagans to Christ look more difficult than it actually needs to be.

Fear of failing to learn a foreign language well enough to persuade garrulous aliens with loathsome diseases to abandon entrenched pagan beliefs has turned far more Christians away from missionary service than Exclusivist warnings about people going to hell have drawn to the task. Teaching missionary candidates that they must trust God to place them in proximity to a Job or two following the initial language study phase is a much more encouraging premise.

Now, please note a resounding agreement that builds between Evidence Number 1 above—the book of Job—and the following array of texts describing God's love, not just for Israel and the Church but for all mankind. First, a quote from the apostle Paul's sermon on Mars Hill.

2. Acts 17:26-28

> From one man he [God] made every nation of men, that they should inhabit the whole earth; and he determined the times set for them and the exact places where they should live. God did this so that men would seek him and perhaps reach out for him and find him, though he is not far from each one of us. "For in him we live and move and have our being."

Paul is describing God's age-long generic providence unaccompanied by messenger proclamation as sufficient to enable at least some people worldwide to "seek him and perhaps reach out for him and *find* him." Surely, Paul did not mean that such compassion on God's part was an exercise in futility. Surely, he meant that Job-like people do indeed respond to divine providence alone by "seeking" and actually "finding" God in regions beyond the pale of special revelation. One can easily imagine an Exclusivist reprimanding Paul with, "That last thing you said will undermine motivation for missions."

Paul, having just made reference to an altar inscribed TO AN UNKNOWN GOD, may have had the man commemorated by that altar in mind as a sample Job-like "God-finder." His name was Epimenides, a man Paul would later acknowledge, in Titus 1:12, as a "prophet" who testified truthfully about the vices of his fellow Cretans. I provide further information about Epimenides in the opening chapter of my book *Eternity in Their Hearts*.

Let's move on to further evidence.

3. 2 Chronicles 16:9

> For the eyes of the LORD range throughout the earth to strengthen those whose hearts are fully committed to him.

Hanani's assertion before King Asa that God faithfully monitors the entire earth so as to strengthen people whose hearts are already fully committed to him implies three things:

1. Such people may be few and far between, but they certainly do exist, and God sees them!

2. Those whom God finds he also "strengthens," enabling them to be, for example, "people of peace" wherever possible. Imagine God changing them into the kind of men Wycliffe Bible Translators' Dr. Kenneth Pike once described to me as "men that other men know they can entrust their wives and daughters to while away on a long journey."

3. The fact that such individuals respond to God as their Creator and are supernaturally enabled by his grace cannot be credited to the mediation of Levitical priests or a prophetic message. Their salvation and subsequent enabling point directly to God working salvifically via general revelation.

In the book of Psalms we find a fourth example.

4. Psalm 50:1-5

> The Mighty One, God, the LORD, speaks and summons the Earth from the rising of the sun to the place where it sets (v. 1).

In the next verse, God "shines forth" (Psalm 50:2) from Zion as he comes to judge hosts of Gentiles whom he has summoned from every part of the earth. In verse 4, God summons neither the Law nor the Prophets to bear witness for or against the Gentiles he is about to judge. What else, then, does God summon to testify for or against them? He summons "the heavens above, and the earth, that He may judge His people."

Thus, God is prepared to judge them not in terms of a special revelation they had never received, but in terms of the witness of general revelation in the heavens and the earth—the only kind of revelation they knew. Centuries later, the apostle Paul would effectually affirm Psalm 50:4 by writing in Romans 2:12:

> All who sin apart from the law will also perish apart from the law.

So, if general revelation is merely informative, never salvific, surely no one will be acquitted before God in this Psalm 50:1-5 judgment, right?

Wait! What comes next? God says:

> Gather to me my consecrated ones, who made a covenant with me by sacrifice (v. 5).

There we have it. God gathers in a harvest of Job-like "consecrated ones." Despite knowing nothing of God's comprehensive covenant with Abraham, God—via general revelation—has somehow led them to make their own individual covenants with him apparently via faith evidenced by some form of sacrifice.

Let's turn now to the Gospels.

5(a) John 1:9 Linked with 5(b) John 3:21

As mentioned previously, John 1:9 clarifies that "the Apostle Jesus loved" was very much aware of two distinct categories of revelation: one that is automatically ever-present with mankind and a counterpart revelation that comes to mankind via special providence. Referring to Jesus, John wrote:

> The true light that gives light to every man [i.e., via ubiqui-tous general revelation] was coming into the world [i.e., to add special revelation to general revelation for as many people as possible] (John 1:9).

Noting how clearly John identifies Jesus as sourcing both general and special revelation helps us appreciate a peculiar chronology in a later passage—John 3:21.

The way John worded this passage is a direct affront to Exclusivism. Instead of opening with, "He who comes into the light [i.e., he who responds to the gospel of special revelation] lives by the truth [of special revelation]," John actually reversed the chronology, saying:

> But whoever *lives by the truth* comes into the light, so that it may be seen plainly that what he has done *has been done through God* (John 3:21, emphasis added).

For the Holy Spirit to be internally enabling someone to "live by the truth" prior to that person's response to the gospel requires that person to be already born of God prior to receiving the gospel (even if he doesn't yet know how to explain his special enabling that way).

John thus provides firm evidence here; Scripture does indeed credit some persons as both indwelt and enabled by God via the witness of general revelation prior to hearing and receiving the gospel of special revelation. Such persons need the gospel, not to initiate their relationship with God but rather to elucidate it much more profoundly. John's description of such people as eager to "come to the light" when at last it is there suggests that such persons are indeed intended, as mentioned earlier, to serve as "first responders" to the gospel. As Jesus said in John 6:45:

> Everyone who listens to the Father and learns from him comes to me.

It is mainly with the help of Job-ian first responders that others who have been resisting the witness of general revelation come to faith when they hear the Gospel. Adding the gospel makes the on-site revelatory witness dual, hence more convincing.

6. 1 John 4:7

Consistent with John 3:21, the same author would later declare in his first Epistle:

Love comes from God. Everyone who loves has been born of
God and knows God (1 John 4:7).

And that same loving God enables "everyone" already born
of him to sense innately that the gospel of Jesus Christ is *the*
consummating message sent to them by that same God who has
already rebirthed them.

Returning to John's Gospel, we find John 8:12.

7. John 8:12

Standing amid throngs of Jews in Jerusalem, Jesus hypothetically
could have declared himself as "a light for the people of Israel."
Instead, he ranged far beyond that limited claim by announcing:

I am the light of the world. Whoever follows me will never
walk in darkness, but will have the light of life (John 8:12).

This claim, inasmuch as it links back to John's initial declaration
in 1:9 that Jesus is "the true light that gives light to every man,"
reaffirms our Lord as offering initial illumination to mankind via
a general revelation that is meant to be followed by a culminating
special revelation, that is, "the light of life." Either phase of that
illumination is one that men can "follow."

8. John 10:16

Jesus himself acknowledged hosts of Job-like "consecrated ones who
have made a covenant with [God] by sacrifice" by saying:

I have other sheep that are not of this sheep pen. I must
bring them also. They too will listen to my voice, and there
shall be one flock and one shepherd (John 10:16).

Exclusivists read these words as if Jesus were saying, "I have other
sheep that are not in *the* sheep pen"—as if anticipating the future
repentance and faith of Gentiles yet to be added to his one and only
sheep pen. However, instead of saying "not in *the* sheep pen," Jesus
said "not of *this* sheep pen." The word "this" implies a "that." Jesus

was signifying the existence of another sheep pen serving as a *pro tem* enclosure, *a sheep pen other than the one at hand.*

With that in mind, let me offer an amplified rendering of John 10:16:

> I have Job-like "other sheep" who do not yet recognize themselves as belonging to this Abrahamic "sheep pen." I must bring them also. As I add to their present limited knowledge of me via my gospel, they will recognize me as the same One people like them have always known down through the ages. Then they will join with these, my "mainstream" believers. The Job-ian "sheep pen" and the "Abrahamic sheep pen" at last will be one!

John's logic in 10:16 is consistent with what he had already stated in 1:9 and 3:21 and was yet to affirm in 1 John 4:7. There are people in the world who, "through God," are enabled to love as they respond to the general truth God has "given to every man," but who have yet to "come into" the special light that Jesus, the advented *Logos,* is bringing into the world.

These, like Job, are already secure in a "sheep pen" gated by the initial revelation of God as Creator only. Jesus sends the gospel out so that—fully elucidated by special revelation—these widely scattered Jobs, drawn in by the greater light, become *one* with the much larger flock. United with the Church by the gospel, they acknowledge Jesus at last as their one and only Shepherd.

9. The Case History of Cornelius, Acts 10:1—11:18

If ever a Gentile mentioned in the New Testament fit the description of a Job in the Old Testament, it was Cornelius, a Roman centurion stationed at a coastal city named Caesarea. As Luke narrates:

> He and all his family were devout and God-fearing; he gave generously to those in need and prayed to God regularly (Acts 10:2).

Keep in mind that Cornelius, who belonged to Rome's Italian regiment, spoke Latin. The Old Testament would not be translated into Latin until long after Cornelius's day. It is also very unlikely that Cornelius was able to read the Old Testament in Hebrew. He probably conversed with Peter through an interpreter. At any rate, an angel who no doubt could speak Latin appeared to Cornelius and urged him to:

1. Send men to Joppa to bring back a man named Simon who is called Peter. (See Acts 10:5.)

When the messengers found Peter, they said:

2. A holy angel told [Cornelius] to have you come to his house so that he could hear what you have to say. (See 10:22.)

When Peter arrived, Cornelius himself quoted the angel as having said:

3. Send to Joppa for Simon who is called Peter. (See 10:32.)

I have purposely numbered the above three quotes for future reference. Why? Because, as we will soon discover, Luke reveals that someone was about to misquote all three accounts of what the angel actually said!

Peter, who was admonished earlier by a thrice-given vision to respond to what proved to be an invitation from Cornelius, expressed keen appreciation for this God-focused gathering he found in Cornelius's Gentile household:

I now realize how true it is that God does not show favoritism but accepts men from every nation who fear him and do what is right (10:34-35).

As Peter imparted further knowledge about Jesus of Nazareth to these already God-fearing Gentiles (who had heard reports of the Lord's amazing deeds), the Holy Spirit anointed Cornelius and "all who heard the message" (10:44) in the same way he had anointed the believers in Jerusalem on the Day of Pentecost.

So let us ask, was Peter sent to preach so that Cornelius could be saved, or was he sent so that an already saved John 3:21 person could be *elucidated by the gospel and fully anointed by the Holy Spirit?*

Exclusivists reply that Cornelius *et al.* were not saved until they heard Peter preach the gospel. As evidence for that perception, they point to a later part of the same story: subsequently, in Jerusalem, as Acts 11:1-3 reveals, certain Jewish-Christian spokespersons criticized Peter for interacting with Gentiles in a manner that compromised Jewish law. They complained:

> You went into the house of uncircumcised men and ate with them (v. 3).

To justify what to that group was his unacceptable "violation" of Jewish ceremonial law, Peter recounted the circumstances whereby God persuaded him to visit Cornelius's household without hesitation. As part of his defense, Peter stated that the angel who had appeared to Cornelius said:

> Send to Joppa for Simon who is called Peter. He will bring you a message through which you and all your household *will be saved* (Acts 11:13-14).

Exclusivists thus claim that Cornelius was not saved until he heard Peter preach the gospel. Hence they conclude that neither can anyone else who is as God-fearing as Cornelius be saved unless someone preaches the gospel of Jesus Christ to him.

That sounds like conclusive evidence for Exclusivism, but actually it isn't.

Reread the three numbered quotations listed above. Luke, under inspiration by the Spirit of God, has already told us three times what the angel said: once in Luke's narrative, once as the servants of Cornelius quoted it to Peter, and once again as quoted by Cornelius himself. Peter, perhaps groping for a way to mollify his critics, added words the angel did not say to Cornelius! The angel did not say, "so that you may be saved."

Apparently adding those few words to what the angel actually said did indeed serve to mollify Peter's critics. They responded with:

So then, God has granted even the Gentiles repentance unto life (Acts 11:18).

Clever Peter knew exactly what to say to get himself off the hook, but in doing so he unwittingly set a trap for Exclusivist commentators who would later misguidedly use Peter's misquote to buttress their belief in Exclusivism.

Here is an example: John Piper is my fellow evangelical. He is known for his passionately Exclusivist interpretation of Scripture. I trust he will welcome my equally passionate articulation of the biblical basis for my Inclusivist views. Without my asking, Dr. Piper placed on his Desiring God Ministries website a cinematic account titled "Never the Same," depicting the jubilant fiftieth-anniversary celebration that my three sons and I experienced with 2,000 mostly Sawi Christians. For that I am deeply grateful. That is why I am pained to have to note Piper's reliance on Peter's above misquote as an Exclusivist "proof" that Cornelius—though lauded as godly by God, by an angel and even by Peter—was still just another doomed sinner until he heard Peter preach the gospel.

In his book *Let the Nations Be Glad*, Piper caps his treatise on Cornelius with Peter's misquote: "The key passage is Acts 11:14. 'He will declare to you a message *by which you will be saved*' [Piper's emphasis, not mine]."[1]

Luke could have easily arranged his narration to quote the angel just once. That he subtly chose instead to give us *three* matching quotations without the words "so that you may be saved" suggests that Luke wanted readers to know that Peter misquoted the angel. Well, Luke, at last we do know!

I submit that an already-saved Cornelius was elucidated at last to the atoning work of Christ as the basis whereby God had already been responding to his prayers. Still, to elucidate someone like Cornelius was very much worthy of Peter's investment of time and labor. Peter gave Cornelius a message he could more effectively use to lead others to faith and to grow in his own faith relationship as well.

One tenet Inclusivists and Exclusivists both accept is that Paul wrote his Epistle to the Romans for one main purpose: to explain and to exalt the gospel of Jesus Christ as "the power of God for . . .

salvation" (Romans 1:16). The gospel of Jesus truly combines God's offer of salvation with something general revelation could not provide: a reasoned explanation of why and how God himself endured suffering on our behalf to procure redemption, forgiveness and citizenship in heaven for those who repent. The gospel thus provides those who "fish for men" with a much wider net to cast.

The vital question is, though general revelation still exists everywhere, are we to understand that God, by inaugurating the gospel, has disowned general revelation as a means of drawing at least some lost people to salvation? Exclusivists believe God has done exactly that, that is, Exclusivists advocate the gospel as signifying what could be termed *replacement messaging*.

Inclusivists, while praising God for the gospel as his "main draw," believe God has not pulled the plug on general revelation. It still has enough juice to draw some sinners to repentance and life, just as it obviously did before. Christ's work at Calvary is still the one and only atonement for sin, but its application is not limited to sinners possessing specific knowledge about details of the gospel message. Inclusivists thus welcome the gospel as *surpassingly amplified, hence immensely more fruitful, messaging*.

Let us now approach Paul's epistle to the Romans, asking, Has the gospel pushed general revelation completely aside or is it still waiting on the bench?

10. Why Romans 1:18 Has No *Comma* After "Men"!

In Romans 1:18, Paul warned mankind that:

> The wrath of God is being revealed from heaven against all the godlessness and wickedness of men who suppress the truth by their wickedness.

Exclusivists determinedly read Romans 1:18 as if it pronounces judgment against the entire mass of mankind. They would be correct if the Greek original called for just one little comma after the word "men." But that is not what Romans 1:18 warns. Rather than warning of judgment against "men, [comma] who suppress the truth"—which would mean that all men do suppress the truth—Paul was warning only of judgment against "men who suppress the truth," no comma! The absence of a comma after "men" clarifies that God's Romans 1:18 judgment falls only on people who, having sinned, as Romans 3:23 avers all do, *continue sinning by "suppressing the truth" as well.*

Again, I am pained to take Exclusivist John Piper to task. In a footnote on page 168 of *Let the Nations Be Glad,* Piper overlooks the crucial absence of a comma after "men." Due to that oversight, he takes Romans 1:18 as condemning all of mankind, which is not what Paul meant. Consistent with what Paul avows a little later in Romans 2:7, Paul was granting the option that—though indeed all have sinned—some men eventually rue their sin and, by repenting, cease "suppressing the truth."

Piper is not alone. My wife and I recently attended a huge international missions conference. In an early plenary session, a speaker assigned to validate Exclusivism as biblical also quoted Romans 1:18 with that unwarranted comma dutifully inserted. So also did another plenary speaker in a later message. Carol and I winked at each other.

Which truth, then, are those Romans 1:18 men guilty of suppressing? The next three verses expose them as guilty of suppressing the truth "God has made plain to them" via creation—that is, the truth that is "clearly seen, being understood by what has been made." They are judged for suppressing the truth Paul describes in the next three verses—*general revelation truth!*

Then, from Romans 1:21 all the way down to 2:6, Paul describes the various forms of evil these truth-suppressor men opt to wallow in. But does Paul at any point flip that same coin of reasoning over and describe what happens to the other Romans 1:18 people who, by virtue of the absence of a comma after "men," God excludes from judgment because they respond to general revelation? Yes! Paul does exactly that in Romans 2.

11. Romans 2:7-11

If ever a passage has been studiously left untaught by Exclusivists, it is Romans 2:7-11. That is where Paul, with no mention of the New Testament gospel included, ardently stated:

> To those who by persistence in doing good seek glory, honor
> and immortality, [God] will give eternal life. [To emphasize
> his point, three verses later, Paul repeats:] . . . glory, honor
> and peace for everyone who does good. . . . For God does not
> show favoritism (vv. 7,10-11).

Just as John, in 3:21 of his Gospel, credited certain people as
divinely enabled to "live by the truth" prior to "coming into the
light," so also Romans 2:7-11 is where Paul is guided by the Holy
Spirit to agree with John that such persons exist. It is not that such
people are saved by their good works; rather, they are enabled to do
good works because they are saved.

Paul thus verifies a faith response to general revelation as salvific
(via Christ's atonement working incognito, as it were). God's Psalm
50:5 "consecrated ones" who make covenants with God by sacrifice—
i.e., his Jobs, his Corneliuses, his John 10:16 "other sheep" and so
on—are thus acknowledged.

Many Exclusivists agree that God favored all such people with
salvation in Old Testament times but they exclude the same category
of people from salvation now just because they happen to exist in
this New Testament era. If that were true, God would be showing
favoritism! Yet, Paul, in the above quote, avers that "God does not
show favoritism." Exclusivists would do well to consider that their
soteriology is long overdue for a thorough reexamination.

12. Romans 2:4

Just as Paul, in Acts 14:17, spoke of God's "kindness" as bestowing
"rain from heaven and crops in their season," so also, in Romans 2:4,
Paul asks the following:

> Do you show contempt for the riches of his kindness,
> tolerance and patience, not realizing that God's kindness
> leads you toward repentance?

Surely God's kindness begins with general revelation; hence
general revelation *is* sufficient to lead some sinners to repentance.
Interestingly, the other 10 versions of the Bible I checked all render

Romans 2:4 with "leads [you] *to* repentance." Why does the *New International Version* prefer "leads you *toward* repentance"? Is this an Exclusivist fingerprint in this popular version?

Further along in Romans, Exclusivists rely heavily on two statements Paul made in chapter 10:9,17. First, in 10:9, Paul declared:

> If you confess with your mouth, "Jesus is Lord," and believe
> in your heart that God raised him from the dead, you will
> be saved.

Of course, to make Paul's very specific Romans 10:9 confession, one must already have received special revelation. Could there be an alternate truly heartfelt but much less specific confession that a man contemplating general revelation alone could make, and be saved as a result? Paul provides exactly that for us by quoting Joel 2:32 in Romans 10:13.

13. Joel 2:32

> Everyone who calls on the name of the Lord will be saved.

From Joel's perspective as an Old Testament prophet, the name of the Lord includes more than just the Hebrew names *Yahweh, Adonai* and *Elohim*. It also includes Job's *"The God of Heaven"* and Melchizedek's *"El Elyon,"* ergo calling upon Elohim via his numerous Gentile a.k.a.s can also bring salvation.

14. Romans 10:17-18

Exclusivists also rely heavily on Paul's declaration in Romans 10:17 that "faith comes from hearing the message, and the message is heard through the word of Christ."

Now we come to a key question: Did Paul intend his phrase "the word of Christ" in Romans 10:17 to refer only to the Gospel of special revelation? If so, Exclusivism has a case here. Or, does the immediate context of Romans 10:17 show Paul's phrase "the word of Christ" encompassing both categories of revelation? Paul leaves us in no doubt. In Romans 10:18, the very next verse, Paul queries rhetorically, "But I ask: Did they not hear?" Answered by, "Of course they did."

As evidence that people in all the earth have at least already heard the "word of Christ," Paul quotes Psalm 19:4!

> Their voice goes out into all the earth, their words to the ends of the world.

There can be no doubt: Paul regarded the Psalm 19:1-4 witness of the heavens and the earth, a portion of which he quotes in Romans 10:18, as part and parcel of the "word of Christ" (v. 17)—that is, a message that elicits true faith. What Scripture connects, let us keep intact.

Venerable John Piper disagrees. On page 168 of *Let the Nations Be Glad,* he contends that the witness of nature in Romans 10:18 cannot fulfill the necessity of someone "preaching," as required by verse 14, simply because nature cannot "preach." Really? Adjacent to the one verse Paul quoted—Psalm 19:4—are other verses that say that the heavens "*declare* the glory of God" and "*proclaim* the work of his hands" and "*pour forth speech*" (vv. 1-2) day after day. Paul obviously thought these communication methods could be credited as "preaching."

Again, John Piper is by no means alone. In that same missions conference mentioned earlier, another speaker quoted Romans 10:9-17, specifically emphasizing verse 17 as affirming Exclusivism—without even nodding toward verse 18, where Paul answers his own rhetorical question by affirming that the witness of creation actually is an integral component of the "word of Christ." Again, Carol and I exchanged private winks.

Now let's turn to another Epistle.

15. Hebrews 11:6

The author of the Epistle to the Hebrews affirmed a simple Job-like approach to God as still effective in this New Testament age when he wrote:

> Without faith it is impossible to please God, because anyone who comes to him must believe that he exists and that he rewards those who earnestly seek him (Hebrews 11:6).

Notice that this verse does not say that the person approaching God must invoke the actual name of Jesus. Obviously, this category includes all of the world's:

Jobs,
Acts 17:27 seeker-finders,
2 Chronicles 16:9 conformers,
Psalm 50:5 consecratees,
John 8:12 light of life recipients,
John 10:16 "other sheep,"
Acts 10:35 Corneliuses,
Romans 2:7 persistent ones,
Romans 2:4 repenters,
Joel 2:32 callers,
Romans 10:18 hearers
1 John 4:7 reborn people . . .

All of these fully conform to the Hebrews 11:6 formula for pleasing God. What do all these passages have in common? They all refer to Gentiles finding God without a single reference to special revelation as something they must first understand in order to connect with God by faith.

I urge that we cease treating these 15 passages as if God the Holy Spirit were only speaking "off the cuff" when he inspired them. The Holy Spirit inspires nothing cursorily. Everything is purposeful. These passages are not to be viewed as inconsequential. Do we really believe what the apostle Paul affirmed in 2 Timothy 3:16? He said:

All Scripture is God-breathed and is useful for teaching, rebuking, correcting and training in righteousness.

Finally, does even one biblical text affirm the salvific nature of the gospel with a simultaneous disclaimer outdating general revelation? In the world missions conference mentioned earlier, a plenary speaker, strongly espousing Exclusivism, offered his audience Romans 3:25 as establishing that very point. What, then, do we find in Romans 3:25?

God presented [Christ] as a sacrifice of atonement, through faith in his blood. He did this to demonstrate his justice, because in his forbearance he had left the sins committed beforehand unpunished—[God] did it to demonstrate his justice at the present time.

A statement that God—anticipating the atonement Christ would later provide—had been deferring punishment in the meantime does not reveal one whit about whether general revelation no longer is or still is salvific.

No matter! Everywhere that Scripture extols the gospel, Exclusivists *ipso facto* infer that the gospel is totally replacing general revelation rather than merely surpassing the latter due to its much more elucidating content and greater potency to persuade. This mental habit of arguing from silence is one that seems to trace back through the centuries to John Calvin and before him even back to Augustine of Hippo. More about that later.

Suppose a carpenter who has been using hand tools for years switches to electric tools. Exclusivists are like friends of the carpenter, assuming that—due to the invention of electric tools—he has once and for all time banished hand tools from his workshop. Not so. His hand tools are still ready for use.

One does not have to be able to recognize a Job beforehand. Just teach your "suspect" the gospel along with everyone else. Some Jobs will declare that a dream foretold a messenger was coming. Otherwise, recognition tends to ensue only after a Job has thoughtfully responded to a careful proclamation of the gospel of Jesus Christ. Soon he manifests a desire to help you proclaim this remarkable unveiling of the God he previously saw only as Creator, Judge and friend.

Confusion regarding what Scripture affirms about special and general revelation as jointly salvific troubles Exclusivists mainly because they favor a few favorite texts while sidelining the above 15 equally pertinent Scripture passages. I trust that by irradiating Exclusivism with the above textual evidence I have unclogged Evangelicalism's soteriological thrombosis on the matter.

Now, as I clean off my lancet, I hope the Church at large will find that what I termed a "seesaw" no longer looks askew, but level.

9

A SMOKING FIREPOT AND
A BLAZING TORCH

Prior to Abraham's departure from Ur, God had promised not only that he would especially bless Abraham and his descendants but also other segments of mankind on a worldwide scale. God had said, "And all peoples on earth will be blessed through you" (Genesis 12:3).

In fact, God would soon advise Abraham a second time, in Genesis 18:18, and a third time (sealed with a divine oath, no less!), in Genesis 22:16-18, that "all peoples on earth" are to be especially blessed via him and his progeny.

God would amplify this already startling emphasis on a world-wide cross-cultural transmission of blessing via a *fourth* iteration for Isaac, in Genesis 26:4, and a *fifth* for Jacob, in Genesis 28:14. That is where God promised Jacob:

> Your descendants will be like the dust of the earth, and you will spread out to the west and to the east, to the north and to the south. *All peoples on earth will be blessed through you and your offspring.*

This oath-sealed "Pentalogue" of promises is now increasingly recognized by missiologists and even by theologians as the very thing Jesus' Great Commission demonstrated was still awaiting fulfillment, not by Israel laterally but by the Church. So—arriving in Canaan, Abraham and his entourage did indeed encounter a pagan population in dire need of transformational blessing. Men in Sodom, for example, were so degraded that even male visitors to the city had to be leery of gang rape (a crime that was actually to be threatened later, as narrated in Genesis 19).

And yet, in a little town called Salem, Abraham befriended a most unlikely king, a man named Melchizedek. More than ruling merely as king of Salem, Melchizedek also served his people as a "priest of God Most High" (Genesis 14:18-20). "God Most High" was *El Elyon* in the Canaanite language as spoken at that time.

In Genesis 14:17-20, Abraham, viewing Melchizedek's *El Elyon* and his own Hebrew expression *Yahweh* as validly interchangeable names for the one true God, accepted Melchizedek's bread, wine and blessing and in return even paid a tithe to Melchizedek, thereby signifying Melchizedek's priestly service as valid.

Still, one can easily imagine Abraham at least tacitly wondering, "Why did God lead me from Ur to dispense his promised blessing here? Truly these benighted Amorites need God's blessing, but this noble Melchizedek is already serving as God's priest among them. How does my blessing all peoples on earth differ from the blessing being dispensed by Melchizedek, a priest who is already ministering on-site?"

Whether verbalized or tacit, that very question was one God was prepared to answer, as we find in Genesis 15:9-21, where a very unusual experience happened to Abraham.

Two Sources of Light Amid a Dreadful Darkness

At God's command, Abraham selected and slew one of each kind of animal commonly used across the world for ritual sacrifices. Cutting each of the larger carcasses in half, Abraham arranged the halves in two adjacent rows. At that point, "Abram fell into a deep sleep, and a thick and dreadful darkness came over him" (Genesis 15:12).

That "thick and dreadful darkness" probably symbolized the increasing self-degradation and spiritual blindness of the Amorite people among whom Melchizedek and now Abraham were residing. Let's designate that darkness as "The Sodom Factor."

Four verses later, in 15:16, God spoke of Amorite iniquity as intensifying but not yet on a scale high enough to precipitate immediate judgment.

Speaking into that context of oppressive darkness, God—who had newly revealed to Abraham that his justification before God was based on faith, not works (see Genesis 15:6)—now added a further stunning revelation: an in-depth forecast of events destined to befall the patriarch's descendants over the next six centuries or so. Following that forecast, after the sun had set, Abraham saw that "a smoking firepot with a blazing torch appeared and passed between the pieces" (v. 17).

Why did God ordain *two* sources of light to emphasize the importance of a sacrifice for sin as a response to that dreadful darkness? And why was the first light source, the smoking firepot, so much dimmer than the second light source that followed, described as a blazing torch?

Ever so cogently, the dimmer light source symbolized Melchizedek's benign but much less informative priestly witness for God as *El Elyon*, Creator of heaven and earth. Let's name that dimmer illumination "The Melchizedek Factor."

In terms of its success in vanquishing resistance posed by mankind's easily affronted and inherently sinful nature, the witness of creation alone (general revelation) compares more to a smoking firepot than a blazing torch. Nevertheless, those who do experience regeneration via general revelation, besides adding to heaven's population, serve remarkably as Melchizedek-like first responders to special revelation virtually as soon as it appears on the scene.

Just as cogently, the blazing torch represented the fuller, much more expansive revelation that God, at that very time in history, was preparing to spread worldwide via Abraham and his progeny. I suggest naming that blazing torch as representing "The Abraham Factor."

Immediately after the two light sources appeared, we read, "On that day the LORD made a covenant with Abram" (15:18). Prior to that day, then, Abraham was like another Job, another Melchizedek. But, from that time onward, Abraham's name would be associated with the launching of a new category of divine revelation, a revelation that, like a blazing torch, would culminate with the advent of our Lord and the spread of the gospel of justification by faith to "bless all peoples on earth." And that is a message far beyond the ken of a Job or a Melchizedek.

Hence, the apostle Paul, in Galatians 3:14—bypassing the blessings given to Adam, Noah, Job and a man like Melchizedek—could fittingly announce:

[Christ] redeemed us in order that the blessing given to *Abraham* might come to the Gentiles through Christ Jesus.

The following Scriptures imply that the priestly blessings God had been dispensing to mankind via Job-like notables was henceforth to be associated with a priesthood named after Melchizedek. This priesthood would continue to be what it had been from the time of Adam and Enoch: a loose, scattered, ongoing "undercover priesthood" with no central hub of authority and no need to be limited to a single tribe or to a set regimen as was the Levitical priesthood. Both the Old and the New Testament acknowledge that longer-standing priesthood as follows:

> Psalm 110:4—The LORD has sworn and will not change his mind: "You are a priest forever, in the order of Melchizedek."

> Hebrews 7:17—For it is declared, "You are a priest forever, in the order of Melchizedek."

This purposely diffuse, Melchizedekian priesthood is still active amid cultures worldwide, preparing the way for the gospel of special revelation. And none other than Jesus is ever working through it to prepare his Job-ian "other sheep" for their eventual happy merging with the much larger Abraham flock.

As Abraham "paid a tithe" to Melchizedek, so should we acknowledge a kind of Melchizedekian influence as preparing the way for our proclamation of the gospel even today. The a.k.a.s for *Elohim* that enable us to designate God the Father readily, and the redemptive analogies that help us explain the meaning of the gospel, are all by-products of general revelation via Jesus at work over ages of time through the Melchizedekian priesthood.

So, then, Jesus, Son of God, as "the true light that gives light to every man" (John 1:9), is "a priest forever, in the order of Melchizedek" (Hebrews 7:17); but as the One who personally "came into the world," he is also a High Priest of special revelation's Abraham Factor as well. That is what corresponds to the "blazing torch" in Abraham's vision.

And now you know whence came the strange title for this chapter.

10

"JOBS" I HAVE KNOWN OR KNOW OF

Only God knows who among the sons of men is truly a child of his kingdom at any given time and place, but we do have Jesus' counsel that "by their fruit you will recognize them" (Matthew 7:16). On that basis, I must testify to the following as examples of people who, in my personal estimation, measure up to the characteristics of those who, according to the 15 evidentiary passages in chapter 8, respond promptly to the gospel because the Holy Spirit already indwells them as responders to general revelation.

I am pleased to find that Matthew Henry, in his *Commentary on the Whole Bible*, cites Job 1:1-3 as evidence that God has his remnant, sealed ones in every nation as well as out of every tribe of Israel.[1]

How sad that Henry avers such a "remnant" as truly present across the world without defining precisely which spiritual mechanism or category of revelation God employs to assure that such will indeed be "sealed" in every nation even prior to the gospel reaching every nation.

Please regard me as endeavoring to fill in what Matthew Henry and others like him say they believe yet fail to account for systematically. I am simply trying to fill in a few blank spaces in the thinking of even fellow Inclusivists.

By no means do I imply that the men I am about to describe merited salvation by their "good works," honorable as were their deeds that I note. What I believe is the opposite: They found the will to do what they did because they were already indwelt by the Holy Spirit—albeit unwittingly on their part—on the basis of Christ's blood atonement for sin applied to their faith responses to God. Though unable to articulate their position, all were John 3:21-ers who were already "living by the truth," unaware that it was none other than God who was enabling them to do so! First among these is:

Kusaho

On September 25, 1968, modern Stone Age cannibal warriors of New Guinea's Yali tribe, grabbing bows and fistfuls of arrows, rushed toward the open mouth of a trail leading down into the Seng River gorge.

"Kill! Kill! Kill!" they shouted in unison.

There Kusaho stood, blocking the trail mouth, arms outstretched in protest. Ends of a pig-tusk nosepiece angled out from under Kusaho's nostrils. A girdle of coiled rattan enclosed his torso.

"Brothers, you must not kill those white-skinned strangers trekking through in the valley below," he pleaded. "Their kind never killed our kind. They have done nothing to us that calls for vengeance!"

The war party paused, momentarily taken aback.

"Elder, step aside!" one of them growled as others closed in behind him. "It is known that the white skins speak against the Kembu spirits—spirits we know mankind must submit to or die. The Kembu spirits may punish us for condoning their attempt to change the old ways. That is reason enough for us to kill them," he added.

Kusaho's silent response made some of them gasp. Instead of stepping aside, Kusaho resorted to an even stronger dissuasion by lying down flat on the ground across the mouth of the trail. For a Yali elder to soil his person by lying on dirt across a trail mouth was the cultural equivalent to building a concrete block wall!

Angry warriors milled about, uncertain. A few turned back, but the others grimly set their jaws and rushed past to the left and right of where Kusaho lay. Kusaho groaned. Getting back on his feet, he flailed his arms in sorrow.

He had failed.

Within two hours, Regions Beyond Missionary Union (RBMU, now called World Team) colleagues Stanley Albert Dale from Australia and Philip Jesse Masters from Iowa—pierced by dozens of cane-shafted Yali arrows—lay martyred on a rocky slope aside a burbling stretch of the Seng River.

One month later, RBMU missionary Frank Clarke and I accompanied an Indonesian military patrol into the Seng gorge. Pausing to inspect the arrow-strewn site where our two colleagues were slain, the patrol continued downstream toward the villaged and gardened mid-section of the Seng Valley, weapons ready.

For a detailed account of what subsequently occurred, see my book *Lords of the Earth*. My purpose in telling this part of the story is solely to focus on the role fulfilled by that amazing Yali man named Kusaho. Two hours later, we were edging along a hair's-width trail on a mountain wall above the rapids. Yali archers hidden beyond the brow of the hill above us were lofting arrows on trajectories calculated to fall among us, a potentially death-dealing rain. Fortunately, only one member of the patrol suffered a relatively minor wound in his back.

Sidling like mites around a whiskered cheek of the mountain, we came at last within sight of what I would later learn was Kusaho's village, Kibi. Every resident besides a man I would later learn was Kusaho himself was fleeing away in the opposite direction. But there Kusaho pranced, weaponless, leaping back and forth, shouting apologies in Yali for the murders committed and pleading like a priest for us to be merciful to his people.

Indonesian soldiers, knowing no Yali, and mistaking Kusaho's demeanor for defiance, began shooting at him from a distance of nearly 200 meters. I gasped to see clumps of soil spurting into the air around the lone fellow as bullets struck the soft ground near his feet. I prayed both that the bullets would miss him and that whoever that brave man was, he would turn and flee before the inevitable happened. Both pleas were answered.

Later, after the soldiers had killed five or six other Yali men in subsequent encounters and set several Yali roundhouses aflame—Kusaho's home among them—the patrol returned to relative civilization with one Yali prisoner, a man named Sel, in custody.

Two Months Later

Kusaho and his family, after long days of hard work splitting logs and adzing boards to build the walls and then thatch the roof of their replacement home, had settled back to peaceful existence.

On the morning of a day the outside world's calendars marked as New Year's Eve, 1968, Kusaho ambled down the same steep trail his fellow villagers had descended three months earlier for their fateful assault on Stanley and Philip. His sweet potato garden near the foot of the trail needed tending. Suddenly, with breath-catching shock and awe, it happened—no sooner had he set his hand to gardening than Kusaho heard the sound of an aircraft approaching. But this aircraft sound was not falling, as was now occurring more often, from a tiny speck darting high above between the highest peaks rimming the Valley. This sound came from an aircraft flying at an elevation *even lower than Kusaho's garden!*

Moments later, a single-propeller Cessna burst into view around a downstream ridge. On board, newly recruited missionary pilot Menno Voth, gunning his engine at full throttle, was struggling to stay above the floor of this narrow rocky gorge he had flown into by mistake.

Menno failed.

As Kusaho stared in horror, the aircraft crashed and began to burn directly across the Seng River from his garden. Kusaho had no inkling that seven "sky people" were trapped inside this fallen "sky monster." Gene and Lois Newman from Oregon, and their four offspring—children ranging from one to nine years of age—had joined Menno Voth as passengers on an ill-fated flight.

As Kusaho, terrified, turned and fled up the trail toward his village, he kept looking back over his shoulder at the scene of fiery devastation below. Suddenly he saw a tiny figure emerge from the only part of the fuselage that was not aflame.

A child!

Nine-year-old Paul Newman, eldest of the four Newman children and sole survivor of the disaster, had found the presence of mind to unbuckle his seat belt and squirm out through a hole where the fuselage had sheared away behind his flight seat. Another moment's delay and at least his clothing would have been aflame.

In a 15-mile-long canyon, a grievous tragedy had delivered a newly orphaned boy from the outside world to within meters of a native bridge spanning the Seng River near to Kusaho's garden. Finding no way to rescue anyone from the inferno, Paul clambered across the bridge and began climbing up a trail toward what he thought were the huts of a village on a ridge high above the crash site. Paul had lost his eyeglasses in the wreckage. What he thought were huts were large rocks festooning a ridge. Kusaho's village lay hidden beyond.

Hiding behind one of those very rocks, Kusaho observed that the child climbing toward him carried no deadly "fire-stick" such as had filled the Seng Valley with thunder two moons before. Moment by moment, Kusaho's terror gave way to apprehension and then to awe that this time he—not the killers of his tribe—could be privileged to make first contact with a visitor from the exterior world. Any thought of avenging the slaughter of kinsmen from his village or the burning of his house was sacrificed at once to make room for a warm and welcoming curiosity.

Discovering that what he took for "huts" were mere outcroppings of rock on a crest, Paul, gasping for breath, sank down into the cold wet grass on a steep slope and sobbed in grief and despair. Now Kusaho felt his awe overwhelmed by compassion. Stepping out into the open he strode toward Paul. Hearing the Yali man's footfalls, Paul turned and immediately cringed at the sight of a nearly naked warrior holding a bow and arrows (almost perpetual accessories for a Yali man venturing beyond the perimeter of his own village).

Kusaho understood Paul's fear. Bending forward, laying his weapons in the grass, he advanced toward Paul with arms reassuringly outstretched. Paul relaxed. Kusaho hugged him, took him by the hand and led him up through a gathering mist to the house he had newly constructed to replace the one the soldiers had burned.

For the next few days, Kusaho fed and cared for Paul Newman as if the nine-year-old Oregonian were his own son. He also used Paul as a living object lesson to charm the Yali people. Gradually, the age-old, deeply engrained xenophobia of the mountain-walled Seng Valley people began to melt. When at last Paul was rescued by helicopter, he took Kusaho's heart with him up and away through the clouds.

Paul Newman's account of the care Kusaho had lavished upon him filled Yali Christians in the next valley with awe. Now they knew who their contact person—their "man of peace"—amid the Seng Valley villages was destined to be. Over the next few years, Kusaho became a primary "first responder," a door opener, for the gospel in his valley. Here was a Yali Job!

Soon after, Frank Clarke, Costas Macris and I trekked back into the Seng Valley. We were privileged to meet Kusaho himself

in Kibi village. As soon as I looked into Kusaho's eyes, I sensed the Holy Spirit springing up within me, filling me with assurance—to my great at-that-time Exclusivist surprise—that I was looking into the eyes of a child of God. I felt stunned. This tribesman of the Stone Age was already my brother in the Lord!

Yet, all I wrote about that experience in *Lords of the Earth* was:

> At the entrance to Kibi village, Kusaho stood, his arms outstretched in welcome. I realized when I saw him that what I had imagined was true. Weighed in the light of cultural differences, Kusaho was one of the most unique human beings on earth! In his untaught compassion toward strangers, his clear-sighted anticipation of unknown truth, and his willingness to differ from the majority, Kusaho towered above his peers higher, perhaps, than many great men in our culture tower above us. Costas, Frank and I thrilled as Kusaho pointed to the place where he first met Paul Newman fleeing from the burning wreckage in the valley below. The kindly faced Yali leader drew his fists against his chest with great force, describing how he first embraced Paul. It was an act that opened a door of hope for thousands.[2]

Imagine for a moment that you anachronistically find Job and his fellow herdsmen surviving today at a not-on-the-maps oasis named Uz in the middle of a remote desert. You have an inestimable privilege. You are able to bring the entire Uzian community up-to-date news of amazing things the one they know as "the God of Heaven" has accomplished by sending his Son—yes, Job, he has a Son!—to redeem mankind by suffering and dying to atone for the sin of the world.

Job and his immediate friends are your first responders. They thank you for adding such profound elucidation to the basic premises that have long supported their hopes. They are also extremely pleased to see previously incorrigible Uzians deciding at last to change their sinful ways as they respond to your new teaching added to theirs!

My colleagues (both Yali and expatriate) who brought the gospel to Kusaho and his fellow Stone Age Seng Valley inhabitants experienced what I have just described by way of fiction as a real-life, inestimable privilege in real twentieth-century time. Yali elders like Kusaho were, after all, custodians—as my missionary colleague, John Wilson, discovered back in the 1970s—of a time-honored code of conduct known in the Yali language as the *wene melalek,* "the ancient words."

Included among the *wene melalek*'s ancient stipulations were homely tidbits of advice for young men, such as, "Do not expect your family to arrange a wedding for you until your beard has at least begun to grow!" One restraint limiting the otherwise almost endemic practice of warfare was, "Do not attack your enemy when he is celebrating a sacred feast."

Probe further and up pops an incipient component of Old Testament law, something "written," as the apostle Paul explained in Romans 2:14-15, on the hearts of (in this case, Yali) Gentiles who do not have the law. That was a Yali rule stipulating under pain of penalty: "Never kill or even wound a man who stands on sacred ground."

Yali culture was replete with places of refuge reminiscent of Hebrew "cities of refuge." Apart from the influence of benign Melchizedekian types like Kusaho, remorseless killers would hardly have bothered to perpetuate such significant mores over centuries of time.

Kaiyo

As surely as the apostle John attested that "Everyone who loves has been born of God and knows God" (1 John 4:7), my Sawi friend Kaiyo decisively wrought an act of love for his fellow man—a deed so self-sacrificial that I cannot credit it as anything other than a God-enabled deed enacted by an already regenerated human being.

Kaiyo was the Sawi father who brought a bloody tribal war to an end by giving not one of several children as a peace child, but his only child. In living memory, no Sawi father had ever made that great a sacrifice before. Kaiyo gave away little Biakadon—his beloved only son—to an enemy father, not by compulsion, but voluntarily; not anticipating material compensation, but freely.

My wife, Carol, and I, under the stress of constant arrow-club-and-spear battles raging right around our little thatch-box of a jungle home, had newly threatened to move away with Stephen, our baby son, and our few possessions, to another village of the Sawi tribe that was living in peace. Kaiyo could not bear to see the senseless violence of his people drive us away.

He so appreciated the way we were caring for the sick. Almost daily we were administering never-before-known medicines to save the lives of men, women and children suffering from malaria, pneumonia, dysentery and yaws—a flesh-ravaging disease resembling leprosy except that, unlike leprosy, it could be easily cured with just one injection of the appropriate medicine—Almopen!

Kaiyo observed also that we were bringing steel tools and other new technology to replace stone axes. We were even supplementing their limited jungle fare by introducing foods and sundries they had never known.

Kaiyo could have said, "Let those who started the conflict resolve it." Instead he intervened—at such great personal cost—for the greater good of hundreds of people. He was also facilitating our mission as best he understood it.

Kaiyo did more than that. By giving his only son to achieve reconciliation between two Sawi villages that had long been at war in cycles of vengeance and counter-vengeance, Kaiyo provided me with a uniquely Sawi analogy befitting the message of redemption. He made it so poignantly meaningful for me to proclaim Jesus as the greatest-ever Peace Child given by the greatest-ever Father to provide eternal peace between God and mankind.

To view the inspiring way the Sawi people welcomed my three grown sons and me in 2012 for the fiftieth anniversary of our family's arrival among them, go to www.pioneers.org, click on "Never the Same," and turn up your computer volume. Though Kaiyo had died decades before, we were, of course, also celebrating his momentous sacrifice, which had happened only five-and-a-half months after our original arrival in 1962.

Though I have described these events previously in my book *Peace Child*,[3] I return to them now with one further comment.

What Job was to the Uzians, what Melchizedek was to Abraham and the early Amorites, what Kusaho became for my RBMU/World Team colleagues among the Yali, Kaiyo became for Carol and me and our four children among the Sawi! Parallels such as these extend down through the ages. Smoking firepots still glow among the pieces of the sacrifice as best they can, but oh! how much better when the blazing torch of special revelation beams in at last, as it did for Abraham in Genesis 15:17.

May bearers of the blazing torch keep pressing on to discover still more Jobs and Melchizedeks waiting with open arms to welcome what is nothing other than the gospel of Jesus Christ!

Tibeluk

My World Team missionary colleague David Martin stood tall that morning. Around him, a thousand Dani tribesmen squatted on a rare swath of moderately sloping ground in Papua's strikingly uptilted Swart Valley. Here's what David was explaining in the Dani language:

"I am so delighted that all of you are saying you want to follow Jesus as your Savior and Lord. As evidence, you have already burned the occult fetishes some of you once used for sorcery. To be a faithful messenger of God, I must advise you, however, that another issue remains unresolved if you truly desire to follow Jesus Christ.

"I have learned that when each of you was younger, a shaman whispered the name of a long-ago deceased ancestor to you. He also promised that the spirit of that ancestor will be your special protector for the rest of your life, provided you keep his name secret in your heart. You are never to say that ancestor's name aloud, but only in your mind whenever you need supernatural help. You were warned that forgetting that ancestor's name or saying it aloud even once would deprive you of that invisible supernatural protection forever.

"The issue is this: Followers of Jesus must trust in Jesus and in him alone. He is a far superior guide and protector than a dead ancestor, and his Name is one you must never hide in secrecy, but proclaim openly. So I ask: Are you willing to renounce those secret names aloud, leaving yourselves henceforth trusting in Jesus and in him only? I await your choice."

Across that open-air gathering, one could hear a sound of Dani men sucking in air through gritted teeth—a sign that they were in the throes of making a major decision.

Suddenly Tibeluk—a Dani elder who had become one of David's closest friends—leaped skyward like an arrow shot from a bow and shouted his secret ancestral name at the top of his lungs. Landing on his feet in the grass, he said to the startled throng:

"There, my brothers—I, Tibeluk, have forsaken my secret ancestor's name. From this moment onward I do not look to a dead ancestor for protection, but I trust in Jesus and in him alone. How many of you will do what I have done?"

Immediately a thousand Dani men and youths launched themselves skyward, shouting a thousand secret ancestral names aloud. The sound of their voices reverberated from one edge of the canyon to the other. That done, they all settled back down on the grass, smiling at David Martin as if to ask, "Does God have any other issues we need to resolve?"

Tibeluk was just one of several Dani "first responders" to the gospel. Later, privileged to meet Tibeluk for the first time, I immediately sensed an unusual depth of wisdom and integrity in his demeanor.

The above men are primary among Job-like individuals I have personally encountered. Over the years, I have learned of others, such as the grandfather of a Kenyan I met named Joseph.

Arap-Sumbey

Joseph, a young Kenyan who had recently graduated from an American theological seminary and had also joined an American missionary society for service abroad, conversed with me after hearing a talk I gave about missions at a meeting in San Jose, California.

As Joseph narrated the following account from his boyhood, I began jotting notes.

"When I was a boy, my grandfather, Arap-Sumbey, took me by the hand and led me to a hilltop overlooking our village and a vista of grassy plains and distant mountains. With arms outstretched toward everything in view, Arap-Sumbey asked me in our tribal language, 'Grandson, do you know who created all that is in this world and in the sky?'

"'No, Grandfather; I do not know. If you know, please tell me who he is,' I replied.

"'*Cheptalel* created everything, Grandson—Cheptalel who lives in the sky but is present everywhere on earth as well. No one can see Cheptalel, but he sees everything and everyone. Cheptalel is good and he honors men who seek to do what is right. I am one who seeks to live in a way that pleases Cheptalel, and I urge you, my grandson, to do the same. Be honest, be kind, do not steal, encourage peace and goodwill. Cheptalel will see that you are doing what is right. He will be pleased and will care for you.'

"Listening in awe, I promised my grandfather that I would follow his example. Soon I began to observe how much my grandfather stood apart from other men, especially from the shamans in our village.

"If the dry season lasted too long and our crops were dying, or if sickness was spreading throughout the community, people would ask my grandfather to offer a sacrifice to Cheptalel, pleading for his mercy. As an inducement, even the shamans would promise to cease their occult rituals for a period of time both before and after the day Arap-Sumbey offered a sacrifice to Cheptalel.

"At various times, I saw my grandfather sacrifice an ox and heard him pray to Cheptalel on behalf of all of us. Everyone was pleased.

"Don, my grandfather died before the missionaries came. I believed what they taught us about Jesus and was baptized. But when I told one of them about my grandfather, he said, 'It's too bad he died without believing on the name of Jesus. He's lost.'

"Later, as a seminary student here in America, I asked various professors on the campus if they think I will meet my grandfather in heaven."

"How did they respond?" I asked.

Joseph replied, "Some of them said, 'No, Joseph, I am sorry to say the gospel arrived too late for him.' Others said, 'We can't say for sure. We'll have to wait and see.' So, Don, I have told you this story because I want to ask you: What do you think?"

I replied, "Joseph, I see essentially no difference between the patriarch Job in the land of Uz and your grandfather in Kenya. Both offered sacrifice to God in heaven. Both prayed to him and supplicated him for mercy. Both taught goodness to the young and were an example of godliness. The sacrifice of Christ that covered Job retroactively just as thoroughly covered your grandfather who responded to the Creator in the same ways as the patriarch. Based on your description of your grandfather, Joseph, I believe we can be as sure of his presence in heaven as we can of Job's presence there."

Joseph's smile expressed a measure of relief.

Warrasa Wange

Albert Brant, a Canadian missionary serving among Ethiopia's half-million-member Gedeo tribe, told me that he once asked a group of Gedeo men, "Do you truly believe that the one you call *Magano* created the heavens and the earth?"

"Yes," they replied.

"Then why," Albert continued, "do I see you offering sacrifices only to the *Sheit'an*, the evil ones, who are obviously less powerful than Magano?"

After a moment, one of them said, "We sacrifice to the Sheit'an out of fear, not because we prefer them to Magano. We simply do not have the kind of relationship with Magano that would enable us to safely turn away from the Sheit'an."

That enabled Albert to say, "Guess why I'm here!"

There was, however, one Gedeo man who was already experiencing a close rapport with Magano, the Creator. His name was Warrasa Wange.

No sooner had Albert and colleague Glen Cain arrived among the Gedeo people than Warrasa approached them with, "I know why you are here. You have come to bring us a message from the Creator of the earth and sky."

"Yes!" the two startled missionaries replied. "How did you know?"

"Months ago, Magano gave me a dream in which I saw two white-skinned strangers enter our valley. As I watched, they set up a kind of lodging I had never seen before under the shade of that tall sycamore tree near our village. I heard the voice of Magano say, 'When you see those two strangers, you will know they are bringing you and your people a message from me. You are to help them deliver that message to your people.'

"You and your friend are the men I saw," Warrasa added. "And that strange dwelling was your canvas tent. I knew about you and I even knew who sent you before you arrived."

With Warrasa's help, the gospel spread rapidly among the Gedeo people.

Yablangba Village in the Central African Republic

In the 1920s, Ferdinand Rosenau discovered that the Mbaka tribe in the Central African Republic had a special name for the Creator: *Koro*. Rosenau and his colleagues soon found that residents of one certain Mbaka village called Yablangba were deemed as more knowledgeable about Koro than people elsewhere. By the 1950s it became clear that 75 to 80 percent of all the tribal pastors the missionaries had trained were from Yablangba village. Via their energies the gospel soon spread far and wide, finding acceptance on all sides.

The Karen Tribe's *Bukhos* Teachers in Burma

Missionary Alonzo Bunker, who lived for 30 years among the Karen people in the hills of Burma in the late 1800s, describes a category of elders known as *Bukhos*. *Bukhos* were noted for teaching entire villages to live righteously according the will of *Y'wah*—God—and to sing hymns of praise to him. They taught Karen children especially about *Y'wah* just as carefully as Arap-Sumbey taught his grandson Joseph about *Cheptalel*.

The Karen people, it turned out, were poised like an 800,000 member welcoming party awaiting the arrival of a "white brother" who would come from the West on "white wings" (sails of a ship) bringing the "white book" of Y'wah, a book the Karen people had lost ages ago.

What I now acknowledge as "the Job phenomenon" was also profoundly evident among many other tribes of Southeast Asia besides the Karen. Those who desire more examples may read my accounts of first responders to the gospel among the Kachin, the Lahu, the Wa, the Shan, the Palaung, the Kui, the Lisu, the Naga and the Mizo peoples of Burma, Thailand and Southwest China, in chapter 2 of my book *Eternity in Their Hearts*.[4]

CONFRONTING "NAME-ISM"

ame-ism is my label for a rigorist adjunct of Exclusivism. In Exclusivist soteriology (the doctrine of salvation), the one and only atonement provided by the shed blood of Jesus—imputed retroactively in response to faith—was enough to save repentant Israelites and even Job in the land of Uz. In this New Testament era, however, the shed blood of Jesus by itself is no longer enough in their view. Exclusivists may not recognize it but it is true nonetheless: for them, in this New Testament era, the name of Jesus and the blood of Jesus occupy essentially the same level of importance in their soteriology. The blood of Jesus Christ cannot wash away a single sin from a sinner who has not believed on the actual *name* of Jesus.

A Sample of Exclusivist Logic

Exclusivist author John Piper drives that point home again and again in *Let the Nations Be Glad.* For example, he states, "The reason [the gospel] saves is that it proclaims the name that saves—the name of Jesus."[1] Piper avers that once the New Testament age had begun, "Paul does not assume that God-fearing Jews or Gentiles are saved by virtue of knowing the Old Testament Scriptures."[2]

Really? How strange that something that for so long had served as a validly salvific revelation for "God-fearing" people could suddenly be totally junked and then replaced by a new model. Piper continues:

What does [Paul] say in the synagogue in Antioch of Pisidia? "Let it be known to you, brothers, that through [Jesus] forgiveness of sins is proclaimed to you, and by him everyone who believes is freed from everything by which you could not be freed from the law of Moses" (Acts 13:38-39).[3]

Did Paul really mean that Old Testament Scripture was no longer salvific, or was he simply denouncing Judaism's anti-scriptural dependence on prideful law keeping? The latter, of course! Paul was warning the majority of Jews who—ignoring Old Testament teaching about the necessity of faith—were focused instead on achieving salvation by their own works. Such would indeed need to believe on Jesus or be lost. However, any Jews and/or Gentile God-fearers in that synagogue who had the faith of a Simeon, Anna, Mary, Elizabeth or Zechariah were already saved!

Pejorative words addressed to a majority were not meant to warn people representing a different category who might also be present.

Consider the contrasting prayers prayed by a Pharisee and a tax collector in one of Jesus' parables (see Luke 18:9-14). While the Pharisee was congratulating himself before God for his fastidious law keeping, the tax collector was responding differently:

> He would not even look up to heaven, but beat his breast and said, "God, have mercy on me, a sinner" (v. 13).

Though the tax collector did not invoke Jesus' actual name in his prayer, Jesus declared boldly:

> I tell you that this man, rather than the other, went home justified before God. For whoever exalts himself will be humbled, and he who humbles himself will be exalted (v. 14).

According to John Piper, presumably if that tax collector had lived until after the Day of Pentecost, he would have had to be re-saved by praying, "God, in Jesus' name, have mercy on me, a sinner."

Again, according to John Piper, whom I respect, even if people without the gospel today happen to supplicate the Creator of all things for mercy exactly as Job did ages ago, they are praying the right prayer but at the wrong time in history. In Piper's view, all such are lost.

As Dr. Ralph Winter, founder of the United States Center for World Mission in Pasadena, California, once said to me, "If

Exclusivists are right [about name-ism], God is like an umpire who changes the rules of the game at half-time but tells only one team."

I have more to write in response to John Piper; but first, some background on usage of the noun "name" in the Greek New Testament.

What Happens If Two Languages Try to Occupy the Same Space?

Cross-cultural sensitivity makes one wary of literary devices transferred from one language to another. Yet, Exclusivist theologians seem unaware that they constantly literalize a Semitic Hebraism that is meant to be understood idiomatically.

All through the Old Testament God's name is constantly used to represent God's person. In Deuteronomy 12:11 the future sanctuary in Jerusalem was to be a "place the Lord your God would choose as a dwelling for his Name." "Name" thus becomes a synonym for "Person."

It is as if devout Hebrew people thought a kind of literary shield was needed to protect God's actual person, but from what? Impertinency perhaps? The usage probably began as a way of showing reverence. Referring to God's actual person directly was too bold—like looking a king in the eye instead of bowing one's head in his presence. The Hebrew people did not, however, regard God's name as a kind of divine essence that was somehow separate from God himself.

As a result, after centuries of hearing the fourth commandment worded, "You shall not misuse the name of the LORD your God" (Exodus 20:7), many non-Hebrews think this simply means "whatever you do, don't use God's name in a curse"—i.e., don't swear—when the primary meaning is actually, "Revere the Person of God."

This distinctly Hebraic usage keeps showing up in hundreds of verses of the Old Testament. Only a few will be mentioned here. In Psalm 34:3, for example, "Let us exalt his name together" simply means "Let us exalt *God* together." Proverbs 18:10 affirms:

The name of the LORD is a strong tower; the righteous run to it and are safe.

This simply means, "The LORD is like a strong tower. The righteous run to *Him* and are safe." The "it" referencing the noun "name" is not meant to be understood as an impersonal entity. Further along in the Old Testament, we read:

> Everyone who calls on the name of the LORD will be saved (Joel 2:32).

This means, "Everyone who calls on God (i.e., truly prays to God) will be saved."

As one should expect, this persistent Hebraism carries forward into the Greek New Testament simply because much of what is quoted or translated in the New Testament was originally said or written in Hebrew by Hebrews. No matter, Exclusivists insistently cite passages that ask sinners to "believe on Jesus' name" as if these passages literally mean that Jesus will not answer any plea for salvation in which his human name is not invoked. Two passages of that category are John 1:12 and Acts 4:12, as follows.

Where John and Luke Felt They Had to Say the Same Thing Twice

Jesus and his apostles—speakers of the Hebrew language—used this natural "name"-linked Hebraism so often that it inevitably carried forward into the Greek New Testament. As a result, the clash of two languages converging on the same message produced a few interesting blips. For example, we have John, writing his Gospel primarily for Greeks, recording in 1:12:

> Yet to all who received him, to those who believed in his *name*, he gave the right to become children of God.

Though John began the above statement in natural Greek, which translates as, "To all who received him," suddenly, in mid-sentence—perhaps remembering that Jews would also be reading his text—John felt compelled to repeat what he had just said in natural Greek, but this time in Hebraized Greek. John's repetition translates as, "to those who believed in his name."

The parallelism makes it clear that these two expressions—"receive him" and "believe in his name"—mean exactly the same! The first is natural Greek. The second is Greek stretched to accommodate a Hebraic literary device. The meaning is identical.

For another example, note how Luke, in Acts 4:12, quotes Peter as saying:

> Salvation is found in no one else.

However, that plain, non-idiomatic statement in natural Greek is followed immediately by another "Hebraized" expression as a way of conforming to Jewish sensitivity:

> For there is no other *name* under heaven given to men by which we must be saved.

As with John in John 1:12, Luke's close parallelism shows that his literal Greek expression and its conforming-to-Hebrew equivalent cover the same meaning. Peter simply meant that there is absolutely no Savior besides Jesus. Blessed as we are to know God the Son's specifically Advent-related name—Jesus—there is no basis for Exclusivism's "name-istic" claim that Jesus will never save a sinner until that sinner acknowledges Jesus by name.

Exclusivists frequently quote Jesus' warning to hostile Pharisees in John 8:24:

> If you do not believe that I am the one I claim to be, you will indeed die in your sins.

Suffice it to respond that a warning given to obdurate Pharisees who were opposing Jesus to his face despite seeing his miracles and hearing his teaching is one thing. It does not apply to sinners who at some point in their lives cease suppressing what truth they know and do what Hebrews 11:6 so simply requires:

> Anyone who comes to [God] must believe that he exists and that he rewards those who seek him earnestly.

That is still another verse where a New Testament spokesperson does not show the inclusion of Jesus' historically given name as essential for a prayer to be answered. That said, all who know Jesus by name, of course, must seek to make his name known as widely as possible. Hence, every sermon I have ever preached in whatever language has acknowledged Jesus Christ by name as the one and only Son of God and Savior of mankind. Praying to free Sawi tribesmen from otherwise deadly curses, I made sure everyone knew that the deliverances manifested were enabled by the power of none other than Jesus Christ.

Once, after I explained my problem with Name-ism in conversation with a professor at a prominent conservative seminary, he agreed with me. But when I said, "Fine! Let's co-author a book on the subject," he replied glumly, "No. It would cost me my job."

John Piper on the Name of Jesus as Prerequisite for Salvation

John Piper, in still another part of his attempt to prove that Cornelius—despite being so highly commended by God, the angel and Peter—was still, apart from believing Peter's message, just another lost sinner on his way to hell, comments:

> [Peter] brings his message [in Cornelius' household] to a close with these words: "To him [i.e., to Christ] all the prophets bear witness that everyone who believes in him receives forgiveness of sins through his name." . . . So again it is unlikely . . . that Cornelius and his household were already forgiven [prior to hearing Peter's message].[4]

One could reason that Peter was simply explaining the content and prophetic background of the gospel, but no—in Piper's mind, if Peter mentioned forgiveness of sins it was because Cornelius was sitting there still unforgiven. I ask: Could Peter perhaps have sensed that someone else in Cornelius's household was unbelieving? Piper assumes it had to be Cornelius who was unforgiven among those assembled in that scene. Piper summarizes, "Peter says that forgiveness comes through believing in Christ, and it comes through the name of Christ."[5]

Piper of course means that knowing the name of Christ is prerequisite to coming in faith to the Person, Christ. That is unadulterated name-ism. Piper seems unaware that if the New Testament had been written by native Greeks instead of by Greek-speaking Hebrews, the noun "name" would have appeared only when it really meant "name" instead of someone's persona.

As another example of his name-ism, John Piper quotes Acts 15:14,[6] where Peter described God visiting the Gentiles, "to take from them a people *for his name*" (*ESV,* Piper's emphasis). Yet the *New International Version* renders the same verse in much more natural English with:

Taking from the Gentiles a people for himself.

But Piper still comments, "It stands to reason then that the proclamation [God used would have to be one] that hinges on the name of his Son Jesus."[7]

Another passage where a more natural Greek usage supersedes Hebrew influence is John 14:6:

Jesus answered, "I am the way and the truth and the life. No one comes to the Father except through me" [rather than "through my name"].

In *Let the Nations Be Glad,* Piper claims:

The supremacy of God in missions is affirmed biblically [in that] ... since the incarnation of the Son of God, all saving faith must henceforth fix consciously on him. This was not always true, and those times were called the "times of ignorance" (Acts 17:30). But now it is true, and Christ is the conscious center of the mission of the church. The aim of missions is to "bring about the obedience of faith for *the sake of his name* among all the nations" (Romans 1:5 [emphasis added]).[8]

Godly John Piper completely misses the irony embedded in his own words. Prior to his incarnation, God the Son was supreme enough to save the Jobs and the Melchizedeks via general revelation, many others via Old Testament revelation and even David's deceased baby with zero revelation. However, now that God the Son has ascended back into heaven, the range of his ability to save is strangely curtailed! Now, as Jesus, he can save only those who respond when they happen to be where they are able to hear his actual name "Jesus," proclaimed by a Christian. By a strict reading of Piper's teaching, even the gospel itself would not be salvific apart from the proper name, "Jesus," being actually spoken and actually heard by a repentant person.

How strange that salvation would be rendered harder to access in this age of grace than it was in the prior era of law. By implication, the efficacy of Christ's sacrifice to save those coming to God in faith is tragically much more circumscribed after Pentecost than it was for supplicants before Pentecost.

How sad that Piper does not see he is actually describing a massive reduction of God the Son's supremacy, not an increase. What he is perhaps unwittingly trying to increase is the supremacy of the Church as God's sole means of bringing people to faith in this age. As we all already agree, Jesus saves people everywhere his Church bears witness with special revelation. But he is also "the true light that illumines every man" via general revelation.

What Most Encourages Obedience to the Great Commission?

Dr. Piper warns that any other view of how Christ saves "would seem to cut a nerve of urgency" for missions. He acknowledges that evangelicals like Millard Erickson (apparently an Inclusivist) "do not intend to cut that nerve. . . . They insist that the salvation of anyone apart from the preaching of Christ is the exception rather than the rule and that preaching Christ to all is utterly important."[9] My position exactly! Piper continues:

Nevertheless, there is a felt difference in the urgency when one believes that hearing the Gospel is the only hope that anyone has of escaping the penalty of sin and living forever . . . It does not ring true when William Crockett

CONFRONTING "nAME-ISM" 133

and James Sigountos [two more Inclusivists] argue that the existence of "implicit Christians" (saved through general revelation without hearing of Christ) actually "should increase motivation for missions [because these implicit converts] are waiting to hear more about (God)." If we would reach them, "a strong church would spring to life, giving glory to God and evangelizing their pagan neighbors."[10]

So John Piper wants us to keep wielding Exclusivist soteriology as a goad, a spur, to keep up the pressure on otherwise indolent Christians until they grudgingly obey the Great Commission. That thinking is light years distant from what I hear many contemplative Christians say when they are as yet unsure about a career in foreign missionary service. As one who has personally navigated the reefs and lagoons of missionary candidacy and service, I have actually spoken with thousands of young people weighing missionary service as an option. Based on that background, I find the biggest "nerve-cutter" for mission motivation sounds more like this:

> Even if I do make it to Xistan, people will still go to hell because (1) I won't be gifted enough to learn the language and culture, and (2) extreme loneliness and isolation will be so depressing I'll get discouraged or, (3) the people will threaten me, take advantage of me, steal from me or just ignore my attempts to teach them while one wasted year after another elapses. And all the while I could be living productively here at home or supporting someone else to go, someone who's more gifted than I am.

Guess how Crockett's and Sigountos's "implicit Christians" (I call them "New Testament Jobs" and "John 3:21 first responders") can help keep all such fragile "nerves" intact?! If a young missionary falters in the language and culture, "implicits" help him improve. They also prove so friendly that the newcomer soon forgets to feel lonely and isolated. And when a Job puts in a good word for a newcomer, pagan Uzites tend to show much more respect and even listen. Ultimately, though, it is those trusty "implicits" who will do most of the long-term work if permitted. Crockett and Sigountos are so correct.

Over these past three decades, thousands of young Christians—reading or listening to or hearing of my teaching about God placing "redemptive analogies" in cultures to facilitate a clearer, even more immediate response to the gospel—have begun trusting God to lead them to various fields. They are heartened to know they can expect to find sovereignly ordained "eye-openers" that can become "heart-openers" among the precious souls to whom they will minister. If just the thought of finding and using a redemptive analogy has had so encouraging an effect, what if I had also been proclaiming that God has even seeded every significant population with a Cornelius-like "first responder" or two? Possibly even more candidates would have volunteered to go find both a Cornelius *and* a redemptive analogy!

Knowing from my own Exclusivist background that a majority of evangelical pastors are just as Exclusivist as dear John Piper, in my earlier years of speaking ministry, it was wisdom—not fear—that persuaded me to limit my teaching to redemptive analogies and the biblical basis of missions. But now, with brave thinkers like Millard Erickson, William Crockett and James Sigountos emerging, I hope a new day is dawning wherein those who have never seen the weight of scriptural support for Inclusivism will recognize it now and realize that I am as strongly committed to the gospel as ever, if not even more so now.

What, Then, Really Is the *Biggest* Deflator of Missionary Zeal?

John Calvin himself opened a Pandora's Box and released a benumbing opiate for potentially missions-minded churches and individuals when he wrote:

> The reason why men have wandered from the truth for so long is that God did not stretch forth his hand from heaven to lead them back to the way. . . . Ignorance was in the world, as long as it pleased God to take no notice of it.[11]

Calvin of course was aware of the Church's incredible era of expansion everywhere in pagan Rome in its first three centuries.

Surely he also recognized that the growth of the Church had *flatlined* from the time of Augustine and his ilk up until John Calvin's own era. How did Calvin explain the shocking contrast between the pre-Augustinian glory and the post-Augustinian blight of the growth of the Church?

He explained it in the simplest way possible: Both the earlier blessing and the subsequent lethargy were what God wanted. If "it pleased God to take no notice," of course ignorance must flourish. If bishops established bad policies, it was because God was not concerned to correct them. God is so supreme that he may deliberately let everything crash so he can win greater praise by leaping back on the scene later as the Great Restorer.

John Piper, redoubtable protégé of John Calvin, says as much in his previously cited book: "[The reason] God allowed nations to walk in their own ways is that in doing so the final victory of God will be all the more glorious."[12]

Piper references two main quotes as proof that God lets multiple generations of people be lost so that one or more later generation will appreciate him better than those useless earlier generations would have anyway. The first quote is Acts 14:16. This verse is so important to Piper's worldview that he quotes it eight times throughout his book. It is very brief:

In the past, [God] let all nations go their own way.

A Bible scholar like Piper should know better than to quote a verse without checking its context. Guess what the very next verse declares?

Yet he [God] has not left himself without testimony: He has shown kindness by giving you rain from heaven and crops in their seasons; he provides you with plenty of food and fills your hearts with joy (v. 17).

Paul and Barnabas in Lystra were emphasizing the very opposite of John Calvin's logic cum John Piper's thoughts. At no time is God ever blasé about the fate of any part of mankind. While people were going their own way by their own free will in the past, as they are still permitted to do now, God was simultaneously maintaining a testimony to himself among them via general revelation's rain, crops, food and joy then as he still does now.

Of course God prefers that the witness of the gospel be added wherever Christian obedience makes it available, but at least general revelation is there to serve as a backup simply because it is automatically present everywhere. So does the infant mortality factor I explained earlier in chapters 4 and 5.

The other key text Piper quotes as evidence that God takes time off for an era or two of indifference is Acts 17:30, where Paul said:

> In the past God overlooked such ignorance, but now he commands all people everywhere to repent.

Context! Context! Just four verses earlier Paul had already averred God as . . .

> [determining] the times set for [mankind] and the exact places where they should live. God did this so that men would seek him and perhaps reach out for him and find him, though he is not far from each one of us (17:26-27).

Paul thus clarifies that God is always implicitly drawing mankind to repentance by overshadowing mankind with merciful intent punctuated, of course, by occasional judgments. I am reminded of Amos 9:7, which reveals that Israel is not the only nation for whom God arranged something as amazing as an exodus! God advised that he also brought "the Philistines from Caphtor and the Arameans from Kir."

Later I will show how carelessly Augustine cited Scripture. Now I find John Calvin and one of his many modern protégés doing the same. Surely if John Calvin truly wanted to honor the Word of God in its purity, he would have expressed grave concern over Augustine's abuse of one Scripture after another, as we will see in chapter 13 regarding the *Treatise* he wrote to defend his anti-Donatist actions. The omission of such protest tells us something about Calvin as well. Instead, he rather uncritically incorporated almost everything Augustine taught into his own theology.

Piper loves to reference William Carey as a model Calvinist missionary. Well, by far the greatest "means" William Carey employed "for the propagation of the Gospel to the heathen"[13] was his own free will, but of course he was constantly in touch with Calvinists and was sometimes confused. He also needed all the support and prayer he could get.

There is, of course, an entrenched Exclusivist power structure behind Name-ism. I regard Name-ism as a fly in the otherwise pure ointment of the Evangelical movement—a movement for which I will always be a zealous advocate as long as it remains committed to the truth of Scripture as paramount.

Why Exclusivism Endorses Pyrrhic Notions of God

Because the witness of the heavens and the earth, profound though it is, omits the name of Jesus, Exclusivism's dictum that the "name" of Jesus must be present—that is, His actual name expressed orally or in print—leaves them logically positing general revelation as non-salvific. This, combined with their indifference to the salvation of billions of deceased children, leaves them content to believe that only a small part of mankind is destined for heaven.

It is precisely this counterintuitive view of God condoning an outcome that lessens his ultimate glory that drives some thinkers, like Rob Bell, over the edge into universalism. Others simply abandon Christian fellowship altogether. Exclusivism and its stepchild, Name-ism, are at the base of this critical issue. These are misunderstandings that have been left uncorrected far too long. I pray that we may outgrow them soon.

What Exclusivists Fear

Exclusivists suspect that whatever truth people today may glean via general revelation gets unavoidably mixed with erroneous tenets of the world's other religions. Indeed, Taoism, Hinduism, Buddhism, Shintoism, Baha'i, Islam, New Age-ism and so on, are religions people like Job never encountered.

But rather than discredit a Job because he happens to live in the context of a non-Christian religion, can't we credit him instead as someone who would still be a Job even if that other religion did not exist?

Exclusivists find it hard to imagine people gleaning insight from general revelation alone as knowing enough to avoid compromising with evil in the encompassing pagan culture. Zealous to prevent syncretistic compromise, Exclusivists thus tend to demean general revelation as granting people in pagan contexts just enough truth to leave them condemned but not enough to draw them to repentance and faith.

Many Exclusivists fear, wrongly, that crediting general revelation as bringing Job-like persons to faith is equivalent to teaching that there are many means of access to God other than Jesus Christ. Not so! Jesus, Son of the God of the Bible, is the sole Source of both categories of revelation and of salvation; hence, salvation via either source of truth rests solely on Christ's redeeming work.

Christianity Versus Islam on the Status of Children

Muslim theologians teach that every child born into this world is born a Muslim and remains a Muslim for life unless—this is the one and only catch—adverse influences in society around him persuade him that he is something other than a Muslim, whatever that may be. Breaching moral law does not end a youngster's automatic link with Allah, according to Islam. Simply regarding himself as a Jew, a Christian, a Buddhist, a Hindu, a pagan or an atheist and so on, is the "sin" that defines a "moment of accountability" in Islam. Assumedly the souls of children who die prior to that transition are regarded by Islam as welcomed into Islam's heaven.

The moment a surviving child born into a Jewish or a Christian family, for example, feels assured that he is a Jew or a Christian, he no longer belongs to the *Dar al Islam*—the house of Islam. From that moment he belongs instead to the *Dar al Harb*—the house of war. All members of the *Dar al Harb* are regarded by faithful Muslims as standing enemies of Islam unless they submit to Islam in a prerequisite way. Thus it appears that Islam does not recognize general revelation as sustaining Job-like non-Muslims in a relationship with Allah. Islam is thus a totally Exclusivist religion.

To learn more about Islam, consult my book *Secrets of the Koran*. While others write about Islam primarily to encourage Christians to evangelize Muslims, without warning about Islam's designs against Christianity and Western civilization, I wrote *Secrets of the Koran* with both goals in mind.

WELCOMING A "CINDERELLA" DOCTRINE TO THE BALL

The premise of *Heaven Wins* now stands as follows: The Bible clearly warns that hell is a dire fate awaiting many; yet Inclusivists find the Bible avowing—as already demonstrated—that far more people are destined for heaven than Exclusivists anticipate. Inclusivism as presented in *Heaven Wins* embraces three major tenets:

A. That all children worldwide who die prior to their respective ages of accountability are included with the hosts of those who receive redemption via conscious repentance and faith. Because of their inclusion, God's already assured moral victory over evil is also triumphant as to numbers.

B. Every person who, like Job, casts himself upon the mercy of God as his Creator just as truly finds that his Creator is his Redeemer as well. All such are included among the hosts of the redeemed. They stand on the earth to serve as John 3:21 first responders to the gospel, assuming faithful proclaimers arrive with the blessed message, and to become God's message-bearers themselves thereafter. But even if no proclaimer arrives to benefit from their help, the Jobs are saved.

C. Even so, we Christians must proclaim the gospel to all peoples on earth just as urgently as if no Job-type first responders exist anywhere. Jobs can neither help with evangelism nor become evangelists until we elucidate

them with the gospel amid the wider corpus of biblical truth. Every biblical text an Exclusivist may quote
to extol the gospel of Jesus Christ as "the power of
God for . . . salvation" (Romans 1:16) and Jesus' atoning blood as the sole basis for salvation is a text truly
Inclusivist Christians quote just as meaningfully and
just as fervently.

Note the contrast here: Those included because of category *A*
above are a large majority of mankind. Those included because of
category *B* above are a small percentage of mankind. Adding hosts of
category *C* believers—the "other sheep" who have been kept *pro tem*
in the Melchizedekian sheep pen—completes the Seed of Abraham,
which is also the Body and Bride of Christ on earth.

Further Cautions

Because we do not know how early a child may develop his or her
spiritual receptivity, it is incumbent upon parents and/or other
responsible people to teach the gospel to every child at a very
early age.

Inclusivism, though intuited by many, has rarely ever been
articulated with anything close to full biblical support due mainly
to the centuries-old opposing influence of Augustine channeled via
John Calvin. Hence, virtually every tacit Inclusivist has found his or
her initial bearings in Scripture via the tutelage of Exclusivists!

Let us gratefully acknowledge our indebtedness. Thank you,
Exclusivist pastors and theologians, for teaching us about the
plenary inspiration of Scripture, the Trinity, the deity of Christ,
the Virgin Birth, the Atonement, the physical resurrection of our
Lord, the Second Coming, the new birth, justification by faith,
sanctification and more. We hold all of these truths dear, as do you.
Know, however, that we reject perspectives on human depravity and
election that oppose Inclusivist soteriology. The image of God in
mankind affords mankind enough free will to rue fallenness and
seek forgiveness.

Time and again, when I teach small groups about passages
Exclusivists bypass, I hear rank-and-file believers exclaim, "How can

it be that I have heard the Bible taught for years without hearing one word about these encouraging texts?" As I have shown already, a significant array of texts affirm general revelation as "salvific," albeit likely only for a small percentage of mankind. Via this array of biblical evidence, may Inclusivism at last debut as a "sleeper" doctrine, a long-overlooked, under-esteemed "Cinderella" perspective, which I hope Evangelicals will at last embrace with confidence and "welcome to the ball," now that its biblical "shoes" are fitted.

Next, I must explain why I oppose, as already hinted above, a dire influence in Church history that is responsible for imposing wrong perspectives like Exclusivism and Name-ism upon the church. Church history reveals how a very influential Christian many centuries ago instituted a strange hermeneutic of Scripture that forced his peers—virtually under pain of being charged with heresy—to adopt tenets that form the foundation of Exclusivism. Primarily because of him, Inclusivism, a rightfully biblical "Cinderella" perspective, has over ages of time been left shoeless in the closet, at least until now!

HOW CHRISTIANITY LOST ITS INNOCENCE

n my first three books, especially in *Eternity in Their Hearts*, I took great delight in presenting positive lessons from various aspects of Church history. If only positive lessons were the whole story! Alas, we of the modern Church must also be warned to reexamine dreadful policies and procedures invented by certain notables who preceded us, including some who are unwisely held up to us as examples of good faith. Heaven's victory over evil is not to be expedited by unbiblical tactics. To begin this section, first note a warning from Jesus.

The Style of Leadership Jesus Commissioned

Both Matthew (in 20:25-28) and Mark (in 10:42-45) record that Jesus cautioned his apostles-to-be with this warning:

> You know that the rulers of the Gentiles lord it over them, and their high officials exercise authority. . . . Not so with you. Instead, whoever wants to be great among you must be your servant.

As for using the sword in matters relating to the kingdom of God, we have a clear warning. Recall the instance of Peter offering himself as Jesus' defender, using violence when Jesus was arrested. When Peter severed the ear of the high priest's servant, Jesus—healing the severed ear—rebuked Peter:

> Put your sword back in its place, . . . for all who draw the sword will die by the sword (Matthew 26:52).

How Our Lord Counseled Magnanimity

Luke records that when residents of a certain Samaritan village refused Jesus' request for hospitality, two of his disciples, James and John, asked indignantly:

> Lord, do you want us to call fire down from heaven to destroy them? (Luke 9:54).

Jesus, siding with the Samaritans, rebuked James and John for arrogantly entertaining such a foreign notion. Some manuscripts have Jesus verbalizing his response with a stern rebuke:

> You do not know what kind of spirit you are of, for the Son of Man did not come to destroy men's lives, but to save them (Luke 9:49-56).

Likewise, John told Jesus of his attempt to forbid a man from expelling demons in Jesus' name because, as John complained, "he is not one of us" (Luke 9:49). Jesus counseled, "Do not stop him . . . for whoever is not against you is for you" (v. 50).

Foreseeing inevitable sectarian branching eventually dividing his Church, Jesus wisely counseled magnanimity ahead of the event. Because human nature is involved, sectarian branching would actually be needed within the Church. A living tree naturally branches. Every branch that bears fruit the Gardener dutifully "prunes so that it will be even more fruitful" (John 15:2). Unproductive branches are "picked up, thrown into the fire and burned" (v. 6).

If allowed to happen, hopefully by reasoned decree, sectarian branching actually serves to keep the Church as an institution from becoming so massive a monolith that evil men become even more diabolically ambitious to commandeer and corrupt it in opposition to Christ's example of servant leadership.

That said, whenever possible, avoiding sectarian splits via reasonable conferencing is of course commendable. Even as early as circa AD 50, Paul and Barnabas, by conferring with Peter, James and John, forestalled a rift threatened by certain close associates of the 12 original apostles. Read about it in Galatians 2:1-10. Acts 15 describes another apostolic conference called to avoid an early rift in Church unity.

The Benefits of Sectarian Branching

Sectarian branching happens not only within the Church but also in realms of science, aesthetics and commerce, mostly with positive results. If just one man owns a monopoly for manufacturing shoes, for example, human nature being as it is apart from competition, he or perhaps his successors may try to increase margins of profit by raising prices while lowering quality. But let an employee break away and compete by selling better shoes for less, and voilà!—the original manufacturer suddenly remembers to mind his soles and laces.

The Protestant movement, contrary to popular opinion, has long benefited via a generally wholesome competition among its many denominations in ways that Roman Catholicism, despite its various orders, has denied to itself by insisting on remaining as a monolithic entity yielding to central control.

The central authority's intransigent refusal to allow competitive branching thus led to religious wars and the horrors of the Inquisition. No longer. The worldwide success of Protestant groups, especially in Latin America, has forced Roman Catholicism to reform some of its ancient habits. Latino priests who formerly incited mobs to injure Protestants and burn their churches ceased all such activities in the 1960s. Somehow it had not occurred to them earlier that such operations would only drive their best adherents over to the Protestants. Competition is mainly a blessing; welcome it!

Virtually everywhere I have been invited to speak to congregations of various Protestant denominations, in dozens of nations, I find pastors who genuinely love and engage with their flocks and are loved and supported in return. Their prayerful preparation yields edifying sermons. Biblical standards are maintained. Love and good will prevail over occasional ripples and extend out even to people of other denominations. Pastors who complain that they are still two or three funerals away from revival are rare. But let us ask, what is required to sustain such positive situations over time?

Every pastor, however godly, can still be tempted to take his people for granted, to grow lax in sermon preparation, to play one more game of golf instead of visiting the sick and needy. Knowing his people are free to find spiritual nurture in other churches is an added spur any pastor can thank God for. Call it mutual exampling.

The liquidity that Protestant church attendees generally enjoy is a blessing from God because it tends to make pastors closely monitor their own effectiveness. The freedom that good pastors have to accept a call to a different church likewise helps to keep congregations from taking their shepherds for granted.

Imagine If Your Church Became Part of a Monolith

Imagine for a moment that all our ecclesiastically free Protestant denominations and groups, by government edict, were forced to merge under a single monolithic hierarchy. Church members would soon find they no longer have the right to choose a pastor based on his spiritual maturity and competency. Whoever the hierarchy appoints must be accepted. Within a few generations, if not sooner, what sorts of changes occur?

Inevitably the incentive for pastors to expend much time and thought in preparing substantive sermons wanes; the quality of preaching lazily diminishes and over time is largely replaced by ritual. Why? Because ritual requires no originality; it can be done by rote. And that would just be the beginning of our plunge into a pit of lower standards and ultimate spiritual blight.

All this to explain who it was that steered the Early Church away from the blessing of sectarian branching it so desperately needed to remain spiritually competent at a crucial threshold in its history.

An Insidious Change of Policy
Initiated by Augustine of Hippo

Over the years, hundreds of people have asked me if I am a Calvinist. I am not. Others have tried to persuade me to be one. I refuse, but I am willing to be friends. (I have also been asked if I am an Arminian, and I am not that either.) Many have asked me to explain my objections to Calvinism, albeit usually in situations where time was too short for an adequate answer. This part of *Heaven Wins*, then, is the proper venue for my response. My objections to Calvinism begin where Calvinism began, in the mind of a man named Augustine of Hippo.

Up until the approximate time of the Roman Emperor Constantine, the Early Church—despite three centuries of harassment and persecution by Roman authorities—remained faithful to Jesus' merciful prohibition against the use of force in the service of God. That blessedly God-ordained policy soon began to fray, however, following Roman Emperor Constantine's decision in the early 300s to align himself with Christianity. It would be only a matter of time until someone within the Church would be tempted to utilize the power of the state to enforce unity within the Church—with the sword if need be.

As it happened about that time, Bishop Augustine of Hippo found himself at odds with Bishop Donatus Magnus who, with a large group of followers in what was then Christian North Africa, complained that the Church was failing to uphold a longstanding code of discipline. Donatus wanted certain bishops whom he claimed had compromised with Roman paganism during a time of persecution under Emperor Diocletian to be disbarred, not from the church but from church leadership.

Augustine disagreed, arguing that as long as bishops upheld approved doctrines, they were tenured and should not be disbarred merely because, in a moment of testing, they behaved less self-sacrificially than other bishops or than noble martyrs in the past. Followers of Donatus—called Donatists—became increasingly vociferous. They began rebaptizing converts already baptized by the bishops they disdained as compromisers. The Donatists thus anticipated the Anabaptist movement, linked centuries later with the Protestant Reformation. They also claimed ownership of church property in their respective domains.

Aha! There we have it! The Donatists wanted to branch off and become a separate denomination noted for higher moral standards than the main line of churches influenced by Augustine. Competition, which could have been magnanimously accepted for the mutual benefit of both groups, was trying to emerge. Repressed by Augustine, the Donatists grew resentful.

Did the Donatists really protest as fanatically as Augustine claimed? Accounts of their doings come only from him and his associate Optatus. Were certain events perhaps exaggerated or even fabricated? At any rate, the protesters were said to consist of six factions, one of which, the Circumcellions, according to Augustine, resorted to violence such as beatings, and burning houses and churches.

According to Augustine, some Donatists even tried to procure for themselves the "honor of martyrdom" by pressuring pagans to murder them in cold blood. When pagans refused, some Donatists, so it was claimed, committed suicide.[1] Could Christians intent on preserving the purity of the Church via stricter discipline be so rabidly deranged as to urge other men to commit murder or to murder themselves? The sheer oddity of such reports bodes of slander.

Dr. Gordon Lewis, senior professor of Christian philosophy and theology at Denver Seminary, opined years ago that "the Donatist controversy was an issue of schism related to Christian conduct" and commended historian John Henry Newman for classifying "the issue between the Donatists and Catholics as a controversy on church discipline." He verbalized the following concern, however:

> Are the Donatists misrepresented in this material, which stems largely from the Catholic writers Optatus and Augustine? R. A. Knox answers, "If we hear little about the sect that is not scandalous in the literature of the time, that is because the literature of the time was concerned to emphasize the scandal; not out of common malice, but precisely in order to meet Donatist apologetics on its own ground."[2]

Finally losing patience with the Donatists, Bishop Augustine placed himself above Jesus' commands. Instead of urging churches led by Donatist pastors to form a separate body and practice their own sincere view of biblical standards, Augustine inveigled the power of Rome to crush dissent by force.

Somehow bridging the divide between the Roman state and the Church, Augustine arranged for armed soldiers to punish the Donatists. Several key Donatist leaders were killed and others banished beyond the borders of the empire. At that the Donatist controversy promptly abated to the level of a grass-roots unrest said to have endured until Muslim armies conquered all of Christian North Africa in the 700s. And that, of course, replaced the Donatist issue with vastly more serious problems.

Augustine's Sorry Self-Justifications

Whatever twinges Augustine may have felt in his own conscience, he soon faced criticism from many of his fellow non-Donatist clerics who saw the precedent he had set as a grim omen. Who knew what long-term effects the violence Augustine had instigated might engender for the Church? A conference was convened in which, according to Augustine, someone opined that "the true Church must necessarily be the one which suffers persecution, not the one inflicting it."

Augustine, seeking to justify the unprecedented measures he had taken against the Donatists, wrote a letter to Saint Boniface around the year AD 417. He titled it "*A Treatise Concerning the Correction of the Donatists*" (*De Correctione Donatistarum*).

Simply because the interpretations of Scripture that Augustine opined 16 centuries ago are still phenomenally influential for both Protestants and Roman Catholics today, I believe it supremely important for all Christians today to understand how deviously Augustine misused Scripture after Scripture to justify his use of secular force on behalf of Church unity. Here are some excerpts drawn from the end of chapter 2 and the opening of chapter 3 in his *Treatise*:[3]

> The Donatists met with the same fate as the accusers of the holy Daniel [referencing Daniel 6:24]. For as the lions were turned against them, so the laws by which they had proposed to crush an innocent victim [namely, a certain bishop the Donatists deemed a compromiser. But the Donatists wanted him disbarred from church leadership, not killed by the state] were turned against the Donatists.

> Augustine thus deemed his decision to arrange for secular soldiers to kill and banish fellow Christians as on a par with despot Darius's decision to have Daniel's pagan accusers hurled to their

deaths in a lions' den. No longer is it only "the rulers of the Gentiles" that dare to "lord it over men." Now a Christian bishop self-righteously wields that option.

With God's consent, human judges duly appointed to enforce secular law may apply a death sentence (see Romans 13:1-5). But no Roman Emperor had appointed Augustine as a civil judge. Nor is it clear that the Donatists had violated any Roman law.

Augustine next assures his peers that what he did to a few Donatists was justified because, as a result, many other Donatists were "daily being reformed." No doubt they were, but the end does not justify the means. Later, in *Treatise* chapter 2, #7, comes this reference to Daniel 3:5,29:

> And the very same king [Nebuchadnezzar], when converted by a miracle from God, enacted a pious and praiseworthy law on behalf of the truth, that every one who should speak anything amiss against the true God, the God of Shadrach, Meshach, and Abednego, should perish utterly, with all his house.

Having newly erased a boundary between the Church and the Roman state, Augustine now eagerly offers both Nebuchadnezzar's and Darius's utterly ruthless despotism in ancient times as a model for the Church of Jesus Christ in the New Testament age. In chapter 2, #11, of his *Treatise,* Augustine even quotes Psalm 18:37, taking King David's use of force against his enemies as a further model for the New Testament Church:

> Again I ask, if good and holy men never inflict persecution upon anyone, but only suffer it, [how then are we to understand] the Psalm where we read, "I have pursued mine enemies, and overtaken them; neither did I turn again till they were consumed"?

In this connection I was intrigued years ago to find in 1 Chronicles 22 that long before the time of Christ, God had already initiated what soon became probably the first-ever by-principle separation between the role of religious leaders and that of political power holders. God forbade David to build the temple in Jerusalem because David had "shed much blood and fought many wars" (1 Chronicles 22:8) in God's sight. The building of God's sacred house was thus entrusted instead to David's son Solomon, foreknown to be, at least in relative terms, "a man of peace and rest" (v. 9).

Prior to Solomon's reign, Old Testament prophets enforced both religious and political standards by, for example, slaying Agag or the prophets of Baal. But from the time of Solomon onward, we find civil (or "secular") authority demarcated from spiritual authority. Those we call the "Major" and "Minor" Old Testament prophets no longer wielded the sword. Only Israel's kings did that with or without divine approval. Even more important—"The law was given through Moses; grace and truth came through Jesus Christ" (John 1:17).

If Augustine truly did not realize how drastically he was reversing God's progression toward something as high above Old Testament standards as the heavens are higher than the earth, every other lesson he draws from Scripture may be just as suspect as those we find in his treatise. Did he entirely forget the meekness Jesus enjoined via the Sermon on the Mount and the contrast Jesus drew in Matthew 20:25 between despots lording it over their subjects and the way his disciples were to be?

There is more. Next comes Augustine's strangely off-kilter reference to Galatians 4:22-31. It reveals him straining even more by implying that Sarah attacked Hagar violently:

> For Hagar also suffered persecution at the hands of Sarah; and in that case she who persecuted was righteous. . . . If the true Church is the one which actually suffers persecution, not the one which inflicts it, let them ask the apostle of what Church Sarah was a type, when she inflicted persecution on her hand-maid. For he declares that the free mother of us all, the heavenly Jerusalem, that is to say, the true Church of God, was prefigured in that woman who cruelly entreated her hand-maid. (*Treatise,* chapter 2, #11)

Augustine even premised the Church's right to discipline members by force as enjoined by Scriptures requiring parents to discipline a child with a "rod":

> For [God] says, "Thou shall beat him with the rod, and shall deliver his soul from hell;" and elsewhere he says, "He that spareth the rod hateth his son. . . ." [So also] many must first be recalled to their Lord by the stripes of temporal scourging, like evil slaves, and in some degree like good-for-nothing fugitives.

In the mind of an Augustine, even the fact that Jesus miraculously struck Saul the persecutor with temporary blindness justifies Augustine himself, as a servant of Jesus, using very unmiraculous— even deadly—secular violence to quell a protest *within the Church*:

> Towards whom did Christ use violence? . . . Here they have the Apostle Paul. Let them recognize in his case Christ . . . first striking, and afterwards consoling. . . . Therefore *the Church, in trying to compel the Donatists, is following the example of her Lord* [emphasis added].

Still desperate to justify his departure from a long-standing norm of Christian magnanimity, Augustine despicably misapplied a quote from one of Jesus' parables: the story of a host who invited his friends to a feast only to find that they spurned his invitation (see Luke 14:16-23). To replace those who had snubbed his invitation, the host requested of his servants:

> Go out quickly into the streets and alleys of the town and bring in the poor, the crippled, the blind and the lame (Luke 14:21).

When even that endeavor failed to fill his banquet hall, the host commissioned his servants again, this time to go even further out into more distant roads and country lanes "and make them come in [*KJV* says '*compel* them to come in'], so that my house will be full" (v. 23).

HOW CHRISTIANITY LOST ITS INNOCENCE   155

Jesus was referring to the compulsion of a rationally persuasive invitation. Obviously he did not mean that the servants were to corral extra guests at sword point and kill any who refused. But that is how Augustine interpreted the "compulsion" Jesus described. Note his comment:

> Wherefore, if the power which the Church has received by divine appointment in its due season, through the religious character and the faith of kings, be the instrument by which those who are found in the highways and hedges—that is, in heresies and schisms—are compelled to come in, then let them not find fault with being compelled.

Augustine thus implied that the Church, with Constantine's conversion, had morphed "in its due season" beyond resembling a suffering widow to ruling as a queen. In all of the above, Augustine's "theology" is adrift. One even wonders if his very mind was unmoored.

Ponder this for a scenario: Had Augustine and others who sided with him simply urged the Donatists to separate and vie in friendly competition with the original Church, no doubt that decision would have led eventually to still more sectarian branchings. These in turn would have spurred bishops and congregations everywhere to honor Scripture and manifest good will so as to attract new adherents, keep other adherents from defecting and prevent further schisms.

Who knows what spiritual health such invigorating competition might have engendered! The amassed wrongs that ultimately made a much greater Reformation necessary centuries later might even have been forestalled.

If indeed Saint Boniface and other of Augustine's peers were reassured by the latter's appalling misrepresentation of the role of a minister of the gospel, what a sad state the Church was in already! Any modern cleric with a "Treatise" like Augustine's response to the Donatist problem in his résumé would surely be rejected from ministry even in Reformed pulpits today. Yet, strangely, Augustine's theological musings are accepted uncritically by hundreds of millions of Christians, including many conservative evangelicals in today's world.

Augustine filled church coffers by offering baptism as salvific—for a donation, of course! Told that unbaptized babies who die go to hell, devout parents soon brought abundant alms. Lest belief in an age of accountability stemmed the flow, Romans 7:9 had to be seen as figurative, of course. Augustine even construed unconditional election as strangely compatible with purgatory! Apparently even the elect could meet roadblocks just short of paradise until relatives paid a bishop to pray them in.

He advised us to worship Mary, Jesus' mother.[4] Little wonder Zanchius called Augustine "one of . . . four legs supporting the papal chair."[5] I urge all conservative Christians to regard Augustine's influence on church history and Protestant theology as adverse. Countering his leaven frees us to affirm biblical support for an age of accountability, credit general revelation as salvific and extol God's victory over evil as by no means Pyrrhic!

Even More Important . . .

Simply by resorting to violence and penning his "Treatise" as a pseudo-justification for it, Augustine opened a Pandora's Box that would soon mar, stain and mutilate subsequent Church history with cruelties.

As time passed, other Christians began manifesting the same ominous psychosis that overcame Augustine. Encouraged by the Bishop from Hippo's uncondemned though widely renowned use of force to "solve" his Donatist problem, later clerics began torturing "heretics" with thumbscrews.[6]

Others who wanted to steal wealth from Jews in Spain easily perceived Jews as even further from the truth than Christian Donatists, and thus they regarded the use of force against the Jews as justified. Soon people who were called "Christians" began slaughtering Jews and stealing their wealth.

Later yet, Muslims—obviously further from Christian truth than Jews, let alone Donatists—were subjected to the Crusades by people called "Christians." Soon people accused of heresy (often unjustly) were dying in the embrace of "iron maidens" or being burned at the stake. Augustine's example of violence even bridged over into the Protestant Reformation.

John Calvin Versus Servetus and Gruet

Eventually, John Calvin, profoundly impressed by Augustine's view of grace as something both God and Church authorities can apply irresistibly, followed Augustine's example by authorizing a man named Servetus to be "irresistibly" executed in Geneva for denying the doctrine of the Trinity. Calvin wanted Servetus to be burned at the stake, but other elders in Geneva chose to dispose of Servetus in a less painful, hence relatively more merciful, way—they had him beheaded.

Jacques Gruet embarrassed John Calvin by lettering a placard accusing Calvin of hypocrisy and posting it openly on Calvin's pulpit. Calvin ordered Gruet to be tortured twice a day until he confessed to his "crime." No sooner had he confessed 30 days later than he too was summarily beheaded on July 16, 1547.[7]

Martin Luther Versus the Jews in Germany

In that same era, toward the end of his otherwise notable career, Martin Luther lost patience with the Jews in Germany and unleashed a violent persecution against the Jews. A virulently anti-Semitic treatise Luther wrote in 1543, "On the Jews and Their Lies," was somehow annotated and preserved. As a result, persecution of Jews increased, justified as having ecclesiastical and theological precedent.

Centuries later, none other than Adolf Hitler quoted (in *Mein Kampf*) from that same treatise by Martin Luther to foment the intense hatred that helped him facilitate the Holocaust! The consequences of Luther's hateful writings against Jews continue to the present, as contemporary anti-Semitic and neo-Nazi groups reproduce his words to stir up and reinforce the same in the minds of impressionable followers.

Thus did all three primary founding fathers of Reformed theology ignore "what manner of spirit" Jesus averred teachers of the gospel must honor. Much of what Reformed theology proclaims is biblically valid indeed; but its penchant for defining human depravity in ways that in actuality negate human free will, thus requiring God's grace to operate irresistibly so as to save sinners, suspiciously had its source not in Scripture but in a grievous character flaw that came to be shared by all three primary founders. Little wonder some of their

Anabaptist contemporaries began dubbing Calvin and Luther as the "*magisterial* reformers."

Seeing how readily Augustine cited Scripture to justify using force, could his penchant for positing God's grace as something that works *irresistibly* have begun as a similar device? If God imposes grace irresistibly but still calls it "grace," couldn't Augustine infer that he was following God's example of "grace" by using force against irascible Donatists? I am suggesting that Augustine's, Calvin's and Luther's "irresistible grace" tenet links with the use of violence that all three men justified.

Anabaptist and Moravian Christian leaders who endured physical harassment and loss without reacting violently all saw God's grace as graciously resistible. They knew Scripture at least as well if not more thoroughly than Augustine *et al*. Nor do we find them misquoting Scripture to justify misdeeds.

SO, THEN, HOW *DOES* GOD MANIFEST HIS GRACE?

As readers are well aware by now, *Heaven Wins* finds God's endowment of free will to finite beings to be the very keystone of creation itself. If genuinely free finite beings could not exist, neither would the cosmos! I am well aware, of course, that the very concept of free will is anathema to many friends of mine. That is why I must explain the following.

Disdain at the possibility that God might somehow jeopardize his control over all things by entrusting free will to unregenerate sinners traces back primarily to Augustine of Hippo—that same North African bishop who used force against the Donatists and then abused Scripture to justify his tragic choice. Could it be that the same man might be found abusing Scripture in other ways as well? Alas, he did.

In the late 300s, Augustine launched another new precedent—this time in the realm of theology. One way he achieved this was by adding a novel twist to Paul's description in Ephesians 2:1 of lost people as "*nekros*" (Greek νεκρός—*dead*), even while physically alive. Paul had written:

As for you, you were dead in your transgressions and sins.

First, some important background. As I explained in chapter 4, two primary events occur at death. First and foremost, the living soul *separates* from the body, from loved ones, from the world. Second, once the soul is gone, bodily functions *cease*. I also mentioned that a cautious interpreter of Ephesians 2:1 should, of course, ask which of these two "death events" best fit Paul's analogy linked with the word *nekros*. The first? The second? Perhaps both?

A "word search" to see how Paul and other New Testament writers drew analogies with *nekros* or other Greek terms for death was obviously needed. As promised, I now trace the word search Augustine could have done.

Paul Also Referenced "Death" Analogously in Romans 6:11 and 8:13

In Romans 6:11, Paul urged believers to "count yourselves dead [*nekros*] to sin but alive to God." Utilizing a third analogy related to death, Paul counseled in Romans 8:13:

> If by the Spirit you *put to death* [Gr. θανατοῦτε, *thanatoute* is the alternate word Paul used in this text] the misdeeds of the body, you will live.

Did Paul mean in the above two texts that we can achieve sinless perfection in this life by eradicating every inclination enabled by our Adamic nature? Obviously not, for Paul clarifies elsewhere that we as redeemed people do not achieve sinless perfection in this life. Instead Paul meant that we, while still able to sin, by the enabling of the Holy Spirit are also able to *separate* our minds from entertaining sinful thoughts, to separate our feet from sinful paths and to separate ourselves from sinful deeds. Note that Paul was referencing "death" as a separator, not as an ability ender.

Nekros in Luke 15:24

In his Gospel, Luke—who served for many years as Paul's associate—records three consecutive parables narrated by our Lord that relate to the theme of lostness. In the third and perhaps most well known of these, the return of a prodigal son after a long separation from home caused the father to exclaim:

> This son of mine was dead [*nekros*] and is alive again.

Not until the Prodigal ended that separation by returning did the father describe him as "alive again." *Nekros* did not signify the Prodigal Son as having zero ability to make a choice on his own. The son demonstrated ability to do just that. Again, *nekros* signified a preferred absence of interaction—an incommunicado state—rather than a total inability to relent. We have a similar usage for "dead" in English. If we see a child sound asleep in the midst of a noisy crowd or a hubbub of activity, we say, "Look at him; he's dead to the world." Our use of the word "dead" emphasizes a total lack of interaction rather than loss of any ability to function.

Ephesians 4:18

Ephesians 4:18 is where Paul stopped just short of referring again to unbelievers as *nekros*. Instead he gave them an alternate designation:

> Darkened in their understanding and *separated* from the life of God.

"Separated from the life of God" is Paul's equivalent of what the apostle John might designate as "not yet born of God." Again, Paul emphasizes separation as his primary focus. Likewise, Paul's phrase "darkened understanding" admits to some degree of illumination. He did not say "without any" understanding.

Augustine, however, cavalierly insisted that Paul's Ephesians 2:1 analogy from physical death designates a state devoid of every spiritual function; ergo, spiritually dead people have zero ability even "to incline toward what is good." However free they may be to make mundane decisions, they lack the freedom to make positive choices of a spiritual kind.

How interesting that Augustine, in his *Treatise* against the Donatists, reviles them by claiming that "the Donatists were wont to cry: 'Man is at liberty to believe or not believe.'"

Could that be an added theological reason why Augustine opposed them so adamantly? Were they also objecting to a primary tenet of Augustine's theology?

Consistent with his misunderstanding of Ephesians 2:1, Augustine proceeded to add still more serious errors to his theology. Reasoning as he did from Ephesians 2:1, Augustine obviously could not view redemption as predicated upon sinners voluntarily repenting and turning to God. If spiritual death signifies cessation of function, sinners are to be deemed incapable of making a spiritual choice of any kind. Augustine thus concluded that people can be redeemed only if God, on a whim, has predestined them to choose him and subsequently regenerates them without their consent. At that point sinners may think they are repenting on their own, but it is actually God doing it for them. All others are lost because God, equally by divine whim, rejects them.

Augustine somehow persuaded himself that the more he abased our fallen race as "dead," worthless and worthy of divine wrath, the more he was exalting God. Yet it is God, as described by Augustine, who is demeaned. Augustine's God resembles a junkyard owner picking his way amid equally recyclable bits of human trash to see which bits he chooses to recycle and which he will simply toss into the incinerator despite their being just as recyclable as those he chooses. That is insane!

If we are all equally unable to choose God, as Augustinian theology claims, that also means we are all equally "recyclable." Hence why wouldn't God recycle us all? In that case, why would God waste anything made in His image? Here on earth, recycling to the max is becoming a new art form. Perhaps we can be a belated example to God as defined by Augustine.

Clearly, Augustine has simply misled John Calvin, Martin Luther, and hundreds of millions of Christians throughout much of Church history regarding at least this one major import of Paul's teaching.

How John Calvin Formalized Augustine's Errors

Centuries later, John Calvin and others formalized Augustine's theology into five main precepts known popularly by the acrostic T-U-L-I-P: **T**otal depravity; **U**nconditional election (which of course requires unconditional reprobation for its flip side); an oddity called **L**imited atonement; **I**rresistible grace; and the **P**erseverance of the saints.

Unconditional election means that salvation is, in actuality, based primarily on luck and only secondarily on God's grace. God's grace operates only for those lucky enough to be chosen by God's whim. Thus God's choice of whom to save or reject is essentially

SO, THEN, HOW DOES GOD MANIFEST HIS GRACE?   163

arbitrary. What other basis could there be—Augustine, Calvin and also Martin Luther asked—for God to spare some and reject others?

"Dead sinners" cannot ask to be saved, and God does not choose or reject people according to inconsequential physical features—hair or eye color, race and so on. So if spiritual death prevents sinners from asking to be saved, salvation has to be by divine whim, because there are only two other options, neither of which biblical thinkers accept: universal salvation or universal reprobation.

Universal Salvation or Universal Reprobation

Both categories of universalism were unacceptable, of course. Augustine had painted himself into a corner. John Calvin and Martin Luther, misled by Augustine, were destined to paint themselves into the same corner. The way all three chose to interpret Ephesians 2:1 left them with no other option. Divine whim had to be the only way election could be explained.

Actually, there is a very different way to understand the basis whereby God chooses whom he will save or not save, and it is one that is both just and quite resistible. All it requires is for us to recognize our Ephesians 2:1 spiritual death as signifying only our separation from God, that is, something we can choose to ask God to undo if only we are persuaded. The key question is, how does God provide the persuasion needed to "draw," to "lead" us to repent? How else, then, can "election" be explained biblically?

In Romans 8:29, Paul declared:

> Those God foreknew he also predestined to be conformed
> to the likeness of his Son.

What, then, does God need to foreknow about sinners that causes Him to predestine them to be made like Christ? Does he, as Calvinists tend to insist, merely foreknow the *existence* of those he selects? Or does God's foreknowing probe much deeper than that?

What was it that ultimately *persuaded* the "dead" Prodigal Son to return to his father? What brought him to his senses was a tightening noose of present misery juxtaposed against memories of an endearing past. Obviously, in the Prodigal Son narrative, the father had no power to encompass his errant son with that effective array of persuasions let alone foreknow what its effect would be. With God, however, that limitation does not exist.

To begin, God offers to everyone the witness of creation itself and—wherever an obedient church makes it available—the appeal of the gospel as well. Whereas only a relative few Job-like persons come to saving faith in response to the witness of creation alone, a generally larger number supplicate God for mercy if the appeal of the gospel is combined with the ubiquitous witness of creation.

If a sinner whose salvation requires that he hear the gospel is born into a setting where he is foreknown to have no access to the gospel, God takes him as a child based on the potentiality of his response to the gospel. This is God's "last resort" option, described earlier in chapter 4. It is also another example of what Paul described in Romans 4:17 as God calling "things that are not as though they were."

God May Add Supplemental Persuasions to "Jolt" or "Nudge"

If God foresees a sinner's response to available revelation requiring an added nudge or two, God is able to put what might be called a "Prodigal Son Option" into effect. In the "Prodigal Son Option," God supplements his primary revelations named above with an encompassing "noose" of secondary persuasions foreknown to guide, not force, a particularly stubborn sinner to plead for mercy. By arranging a fortuitous sequence of events, friendships, twinges of conscience, disappointments, sickness, crises, setbacks, giftings or bereavements that God foreknows will, over time, elicit a freewill supplication by the sinner, God "predestines" him or her by arranging it all!

God's provision of *generic* revelation corresponds to Jesus saying, "Many are invited" (Matthew 22:14). His added comment that "few are chosen" corresponds to God adding *accessory* persuasions only when responses foreseen as potential are invited to happen in real time.

Granted, there is also an opposing force. Writing to the Church at Corinth, the apostle Paul described the deceptive nature of the evil one:

The god of this age has blinded the minds of unbelievers, so they cannot see the light of the gospel (2 Corinthians 4:4).

Still, if the Holy Spirit's persuasive "jolts" are sufficiently vigorous, a crack opens, allowing enough light to beam through. A freewill response foreseen by God is thus elicited. Via God's foreknown effective persuasions, supplicants are thus predestined to be made like Christ (since God knows in advance that he or she will repent and be saved). Note: When stubborn people unwittingly stumble across their foreknown thresholds of submission and pray to be saved, they do so of their own free will, yes, but that happens only in response to persuasions God has to foreknow and sovereignly orchestrate. As soon as the mind, heart and will surrender to God, salvation ensues followed by the peace, joy and enabling grace that attend citizens of God's kingdom.

Please note that the persuasions God employs in this life are always such that individuals who respond to them know that they still *could* choose to say no. In the next life, the persuasions God uses will not be to offer salvation but to prohibit evil. Those persuasions, described in several Scriptures cited earlier, will not be so gentle.

I submit that it was on the basis of these more complex categories of foreknowledge that Jesus could claim:

All that the Father gives me will come to me, and whoever comes to me I will never drive away (John 6:37).

It's as if the Prodigal's father was able to do much more than simply await his son's return. It's as if he, from a distance, knew how to mesh persuasions together so as to draw his son back from that "far country."

Observe how truly the above operation is all of grace. Grace gave existence to the sinner in the first place. Grace provided both the primary revelations and the accessory persuasions needed to draw him to God. Grace gifted the sinner with the free will that he was foreknown to use appropriately amid a God-orchestrated set of persuasions. And God's grace accomplishes all these things without nullifying the image of God, which James 3:9 assures us is still present in the nature of man despite the Fall.

The sinner thus has no basis to brag at all, but only to be grateful! Paul's Ephesians chapter 2 stipulations are all satisfied.

Scripture Also Mentions *Goading*

In Acts 9, nudging apparently failed, so God applied goading to achieve the desired effect. Paul confessed before King Agrippa in Acts 26:14 that he, years before—lying blinded on the road to Damascus—heard Jesus reprove him for two offenses: (1) persecuting Jesus, and (2) kicking against "the goads." The memory of Stephen praying as Paul's peers were slaying him, saying, "Lord, do not hold this sin against them" (Acts 7:60), was probably just one of several "goads" Jesus used to render Paul susceptible for that extremely dramatic Acts chapter 9 conversion experience.

What If Even *Goading* Is Foreknown to Fail?

What if God "scans" another individual's finite social context only to find that no matter what may be contrived for his benefit, he will stubbornly spurn every persuasion, both primary and accessory? Surely we cannot expect that God will extend that person's life inordinately, for example, or intervene in a way that is unfair toward other people for the sake of one who is persistently obdurate. Such individuals ordain themselves to die in their sins and face the eternal consequences. Foreseeing their self-inflicted fate, God may do no arranging at all for them, unless perhaps to benefit others through them or enable them to procreate descendants God foreknows will one day come into his kingdom. By their own choice, all such persons limit their own destinies as non-elect "object[s] of [God's] wrath—prepared for destruction" (Romans 9:22).

And that is how I posit we may best understand what Paul meant by "whom he foreknew he also predestined." This is a foreknowledge based not upon arbitrary divine whim, but upon divine foresight of a potential freewill repentance that God discovers can be made actual within the finite context of a sinner's life and times. Sinners never make any such freewill choice unaided, but only in response to persuasions God foreknows and guarantees at precise places at precisely foreknown opportune moments. Ergo no sinner who finds salvation has any basis to boast!

Rejecting the above approach to what predestination means, Calvinist author/teacher/pastor R. C. Sproul, for example, wrote an entire volume titled *Willing to Believe*[1] to deny that sinners have the slightest ability to will to do any such thing as repent or believe or anything else that might give God basis to elect them for salvation. In defending the cessation-of-function notion of spiritual death, Sproul argued that one does not stand in a graveyard and ask if those buried in one area are less dead than those buried elsewhere. So also all who are spiritually dead, according to Sproul, are equally unable to choose God. He also criticized evangelist Billy Graham for asking sinners to repent and believe, activities that spiritually dead sinners have zero ability to perform, according to Dr. Sproul. How else, then, does one "do the work of an evangelist" (2 Timothy 4:5)?

Sproul has no inkling that if only Augustine and Calvin had done what scholars call a careful "word search" to discover by consensus how New Testament writers intended analogies based on *nekros* and *thanatoute* to be understood, Sproul's own teachings would be quite different. Augustine, Calvin and others who followed their line of interpretation simply breezed past the initial event—the fact that death *separates* the soul from the body, from loved ones, from the world. Their decision to focus instead on cessation of function, a secondary event at the moment of death, set the mold for Reformed theology's doctrines called "total depravity," "unconditional election" and "irresistible grace."

Does God Irresistibly Force Himself upon Us or Does He *Draw* Us?

Though sinners are indeed "dead" by virtue of their separation from God, they have the potential—like the Prodigal Son—to be persuaded to repent. It is far and away plightful enough that sinners cannot free themselves from sin, cannot atone for their sin, cannot save themselves and cannot rid themselves of the Adamic nature. Adding to these obvious "cannots" by claiming that sinners lack the freedom even "to incline toward what is good" was totally unjustified and misleading.

I asked a certain evangelical pastor why he had decided to accept the tenets of Reformed theology. He responded, "I began to feel that my concept of God was too small. Reformed theology helped me see God as much bigger."

I replied, "Previously, you saw God as so consummately sovereign that he could grant genuine free will to billions of people while still overruling all the consequences, securing the Church, conquering evil and shepherding history to its appointed end. Now you believe in a God who wouldn't dare jeopardize his sovereignty by turning all that free will loose. I ask you, my friend, which view sees God as bigger?"

Brothers and sisters in Christ, nowhere does the Bible speak of God irresistibly regenerating sinners so as to facilitate their subsequent repentance, or of saving them so they can then "ask" to be saved. I recall hearing Southern Baptist Pastor Adrian Rogers rebutting Augustine by describing how Jesus, God the Son, was so grieved over Jewish ability to resist his will that he wept, saying:

> O, Jerusalem, Jerusalem, you who kill the prophets and stone those sent to you, how often I have longed to gather your children together, as a hen gathers her chicks under her wings, but you were not willing (Matthew 23:37; see also Luke 13:34).

Jesus did not overpower their unwillingness, nor does he overpower yours and mine. Again and again the Bible speaks of an opposite process in which repentance and regeneration are preceded by an initial phase in which God is described as "drawing" or "leading" sinners to repent, which of course means that they are able to resist or respond to his drawing. Only if they respond are they brought to new birth. Here are four examples:

> No one can come to me unless the Father who sent me draws him (John 6:44).

> But I, when I am lifted up from the earth, will draw all men to myself (John 12:32).

> God's kindness leads you toward repentance (Romans 2:4).

I stand at the door and knock [rather than "kick it in"!]. If anyone hears my voice and opens the door, I will come in (Revelation 3:20).

Lest anyone think the above distinction doesn't matter, it does! Inevitably, if one key principle in Scripture is misinterpreted, other things will begin to go wrong in the Christian experience of people affected by the initial error.

Early in my walk with Christ, I began to see the Augustinian/ Calvinist notion of unconditional election and irresistible grace— integral components of Reformed theology—as potentially afflicting Christians with an eerie spiritual thrombosis. It took me years to trace the source of the problem to Augustine's misreading of Ephesians 2:1. Let me explain why my search began.

My Own Extended Family's Personal Experience: What Can Happen When Calvinism Is Carried to Its Logical Extreme

My dear mother (now with the Lord) was one of 13 children raised under the influence of a Free Church of Scotland church in Argyle Shore, Prince Edward Island, Canada. A series of pastors, applying Calvinism to the max, taught the congregation that asking God to save you would be rather presumptuous. God saves only those whom he chooses to save. If he has not chosen you, there is no eternal hope for you. Conversely, if he has chosen to save you, you will know it because a moment will come when you will "see the light and overflow with joy."

Only a certain percentage of church members—my grandmother being one—appeared to be so conspicuously blessed. The rest of the congregation languished in envy, waited in hope or remained indifferent. One by one, all 13 Stewart children, including my mother, grew up and left that church without "seeing the light." Only three, who were dying of tuberculosis, showed signs of knowing God in their youth, and that was after they had to leave the church to await death in a sanitarium in Charlottetown.

I suspect the three facing death simply ignored their pastor's counsel by praying, however "presumptuously," to be saved! Good for them! Only one of my mother's many siblings, plus a widowed spouse of another, did I ever hear give testimony of receiving Christ—and that was because of the ministry of non-Reformed evangelical churches. Other of my mother's siblings died relatively young as unbelievers. Two were alcoholics.

My own mother did not receive Christ until I, at 17 years of age, led her to him. New to the faith myself at the time, I was amazed to discover how little she knew about the Bible, given her background. Clearly, Calvinist theology had persuaded my godly grandmother that inviting her children to pray, one by one, to receive Jesus as their Lord and Savior would be a vain attempt to preempt divine sovereignty. Thank God my Mother lived out the rest of her life as a happy believer in Christ! But I still grieve over the Calvinist theology in that bound and tethered church—misnamed as "free"—that failed to invite my mother and my numerous aunts and uncles to experience salvation simply by supplicating God for mercy, especially at an early age.

By and large, the members of that ultra-Reformed congregation were practical, hardworking, common-sense people of good will who were not even dimly aware that the theology they took pride in was inhibiting them from fulfilling what the apostle Paul enjoined of Timothy:

Do the *work* of an evangelist (2 Timothy 4:5).

Whereas other churches lose their spiritual dynamic under liberal theology, the Free Church of Scotland, which broke away from the Church of Scotland in 1843, was by no means liberal! In Argyle Shore, Prince Edward Island, at least, it was dying instead under the stultifying blight of an unfortunate sidetrack of conservative theology known as "hyper-Calvinism"—Reformed theology on steroids, so to speak.

Hyper-Calvinism's Antipathy Toward Both Evangelicals and Evangelism

Thank God, the aggression resorted to by Augustine, Calvin and Luther centuries ago, described earlier, is no longer so apparent under the banner of Reformed theology today, except for one small trace. The demeaning attitude that certain hard-core hyper-Calvinists manifest toward non-Calvinist evangelicals is often quite repelling. They snidely accuse other Christians of "exalting the creature above the Creator" when no such thing is intended. That is not to say that a majority of Calvinists are "hyper-Calvinists."

Years ago, a promising seminary graduate joined World Team— the interdenominational faith mission that sponsored my first wife and me to work among Papua's Sawi tribespeople. Fully supported by churches that shared our esteem for his potential, the new recruit was awaiting his flight to Indonesia when someone handed him a book written by a hyper-Calvinist. By the time our new colleague landed on the far side of the Pacific Ocean, that book had persuaded him to catch the next flight back to America.

That promising young man shocked World Team's welcoming party on the field by asserting that persuading existing non-Reformed American churches to honor John Calvin's theology was far more important than winning the lost to Christ in a Muslim nation like Indonesia. (Apparently, angels in heaven exult much more over an already born-again evangelical Christian converting to Calvinism than over a Muslim or a pagan redeemed by the gospel.) Unconditional election and irresistible grace—amply able to guarantee the conversion of the lost—apparently need lots of human help when it comes to compelling other Christians to accept Calvinism's "five points." That apparently is why hyper-Calvinists prefer to leave reaching the lost entirely to God while they focus their own energies on converting fellow Christians to Calvinism.

That may be what Kenneth Stewart, Professor of Theological Studies at Covenant College, had in mind when he responded to a question about hyper-Calvinism in an interview for *Credo Magazine*. Stewart spoke of "an old attitude . . . that—since God is free to do all things—He might also have a way of saving those beyond [the reach of the Church]." Stewart went on to claim that "this is no time for evangelical Calvinists" to rest on "the bare historical record" of the past.[2]

Stewart's willingness to distinguish evangelical Calvinists from Calvinists in general is refreshingly candid.

Emulating a strategy also favored by Jehovah's Witnesses and Mormons, one ultra-Reformist group I met sends its teachers abroad, not to win the lost but to indoctrinate third-world evangelical Christians, especially pastors, with hyper-Calvinism.

Years ago, standing by my display at a missions conference in a strongly Reformed church in Tempe, Arizona, I observed a display next to mine featuring a Reformed mission serving in Mexico. I asked the young couple in charge of the display what was their mission's primary goal in Mexico—urban church-planting? Indian tribes? Their immediate brazen response was, "Neither! Our task is to persuade evangelical Mexican pastors to teach Calvinism in already existing Mexican churches."

Extending the kingdom of God by evangelizing the lost would have been a nuisance distraction from their primary goal: converting evangelical Christians to "five-point Calvinism."

For years, I thought (and hoped) that the mission that young couple represented was only a small offshoot from the main thrust of Reformed missionary endeavor. Now I am not so sure. At a recent large-scale Reformed missions conference I attended out of curiosity, the music was worshipful and most of the preaching was substantive in content, passionate and inspiring. National converts from other countries testified of God's work in "hard-to-reach" areas. John Piper and other speakers urged the Church to focus primarily on reaching the more than 3,000 not only unreached but also "unengaged" people groups still remaining worldwide. Everything was so winsomely packaged. I thought, *How encouraging! Surely this is what Dr. Kenneth Stewart must mean by "evangelical Calvinism."*

But then I attended a breakout session taught by a Reformed pastor from Latin America. The title of his presentation was "Why Latin America Needs to Be 'Re-evangelized.'" The thrust of his lecture was to persuade Calvinist missionaries in Latin America to focus their energies on re-converting those he regarded as pseudo-Christian Latino Pentecostals and evangelicals to Calvinism.

During the last 30 years, I have been privileged to speak to dozens of evangelical congregations in major cities of Brazil, Mexico and Chile, and in one or two conferences each in Venezuela, El Salvador, Jamaica and Barbados. So I was very eager to examine this Reformed pastor's premise. I was also curious to know how re-evangelizing South America, Mexico and the Caribbean Islands could help the Church reach the more than 3,000 "unengaged" people groups we had been hearing about in the plenary sessions.

The speaker began by describing how various evangelicals who attained high levels of political office in Guatemala, Peru and other Latin nations failed totally to transform their societies (as if that could happen in the brief span of a few years in office in predominantly Roman Catholic nations).

He also claimed that the Pentecostal majority among Latin American Protestants has succumbed to prosperity theology's "false gospel" and hence may be deemed as not truly born again but lost and needing Calvinism's "true gospel."

Third, he claimed that most other non-Reformed and non-Pentecostal Latino evangelicals are also deceived into thinking they are saved because they prayed a wrongly worded "sinner's prayer" urged upon them in the form of "The Four Spiritual Laws" developed by Campus Crusade for Christ (now called "Cru" in the USA). The speaker capped his summary of the four spiritual laws with a strongly worded claim that the four laws urge sinners to ask for forgiveness "without first repenting of their sins." No repentance leads to no forgiveness, hence false hope. The speaker appealed for missionaries (some of whom might otherwise go to unengaged, unreached pagans) to help instead with the task of "re-evangelizing" Latin American Pentecostals and evangelicals, presumably by teaching the only kind of theology that in his mind is truly biblical—Reformed theology.

So, for that long ago seminary graduate to turn his back on lost Muslims in Indonesia to convert Christians to Calvinism in America apparently was not such an odd thing after all, even in the most promisingly energized Calvinist circles!

But did that workshop speaker ever read the way the four spiritual laws are actually worded? Apparently he did not. Laws 1 through 3 clearly describe sin as the problem that created a barrier between God and man, the inability of good works or human effort to bridge that "gulf," and God's only remedy for sin provided via the atonement of Jesus Christ. Detailed diagrams are provided to complement scriptural quotations. Following articulation of the first three Laws, Campus Crusade for Christ presents the fourth Law as follows. Note the inclusion of the word "repentance."

Law 4
We must individually receive Jesus Christ as Savior and Lord; then we can know and experience God's love and plan for our lives.

We Must Receive Christ
"As many as received Him, to them He gave the right to become children of God, to those who believe in His name"
(John 1:12, NKJV).

We Receive Christ Through Faith
"By grace you have been saved through faith; and that not of yourselves; it is the gift of God; not of works, lest anyone should boast" (Ephesians 2:8,9, NKJV).

When We Receive Christ, We Experience a New Birth
(Read John 3:1-8.)

We Receive Christ Through Personal Invitation
[Christ speaking] "Behold, I stand at the door and knock. If any one hears My voice and opens the door, I will come in to him" (Revelation 3:20, NKJV).

Receiving Christ involves turning to God from self (repentance) and trusting Christ to come into our lives to forgive our sins and to make us what He wants us to be.

Just to agree intellectually that Jesus Christ is the Son of God and that He died on the cross for our sins is not enough. Nor is it enough to have an emotional experience. We receive Jesus Christ by faith, as an act of the will.

A subsequent diagram on Cru's website and in their printed booklets describes the difference between the self-directed life and the Christ-directed life.[3]

It would not be at all surprising if some of the speaker's audience in that packed room may have found Christ through The Four Spiritual Laws and even used the same to lead others to Christ. Even so, a number of hearty "amens" resounded from several listeners eager to agree that evangelism that is not specifically based on Reformed theology is a false evangelism that Reformed Christians are obligated to supersede.

I thought of Jesus' parable recorded in Matthew 13:24-30 about an enemy sowing weeds amid the farmer's wheat. In that parable, his solution was to let the wheat and the weeds grow together until the harvest, at which time they would be separated much more expediently. That of course would allow the farmer meanwhile to plant and harvest other fields!

Granting that "prosperity theology" is a "weed-sowing" influence, surely it is massively wrong to sideline the task of evangelizing millions of totally unreached people so as to focus judgmentally on millions of others, many of whom I personally know are actively preaching the gospel and seeing lives transformed. Would not honoring the primary goal of that conference by penetrating totally unengaged, unreached people groups with the gospel be a far more worthy venture?

I grieve at how readily that Reformed pastor could brand prosperity theology-obsessed Pentecostals and regular evangelical Christians with the same hot iron. He demeaned as unbelievers the tens of thousands of vibrant Latino believers such as those I have personally met, and hosts of others like them. That includes hundreds of young Brazilians venturing abroad to places like Mozambique and even to various Muslim nations as career missionaries. I wonder also how many attendees of that workshop are even now repeating that speaker's charges against such.

Thus, even in a massive conference promoting impressively "evangelical" Calvinism, valid anti-prosperity theology sentiment segues to animus against non-Reformed evangelical churches, evangelistic methods and even evangelical mission agencies.

I also sat there weighing an inherent irony. Whereas Reformed authors and radio personalities purport that sinners are simply unable to repent until irresistible grace forces repentance into their hearts, here was another Reformed pastor advising that saying a prayer of repentance with certain words missing turns God's grace away. Obviously, if an R. C. Sproul is right, words spoken beforehand don't matter, because repentance never occurs prior to salvation anyway.

Another Example of Hyper-Calvinist "Stultification"

A close friend of mine in Cincinnati, having imbibed Calvinism up to his gills, separated himself from Evangelical circles. Forming his own reclusive house church, he kept regurgitating his Calvinist convictions year after year with a clique of about one dozen people. Not once did I ever hear him talk about outreach to unbelievers. His main mission in life was to hand out or mail literature on Calvinism, especially books by Arthur Pink, to already mature Christians. His focus resembled a cultic obsession. I believe he and his flock—a group of spiritually alive people, no doubt—could have experienced growth in numbers apart from hyper-Calvinism's stultifying effect.

Based on my personal observation, many members of "balanced" Reformed churches have never met a hyper-Calvinist and are quite unaware that the Calvinism they themselves espouse—absorbed fixatedly—has the potential to morph even "balanced" Christians into the hyper-Calvinist mold.

Yet certain Reformed authors and radio personalities keep claiming that Reformed theology rightly holds the highest intellectual ground in Christendom. Far from it! Reformed theology, quite frankly, was ill founded by three notable Christians who failed tragically to maintain a Christ-like spirit to the end of their lives. Any modern pastoral candidate with a résumé similar to the ones Augustine, Calvin and Luther died with would not qualify to pastor even a Reformed Bible-believing church in today's world. I question whether even hyper-Calvinists would accept them as pastors.

Evaluating the Classical Reformers via their writings is problematic enough. Add their historically recorded misdeeds and the perspective darkens yet more. To their credit, the churches Calvin and Luther founded did indeed teach justification by faith at least until, centuries later, the camel of liberalism began to get its head inside the tent of certain denominations traced to their influence. Thank God that Luther translated the Bible into German. Thank

God for all the good things the "Classical" Reformers did. But they also failed God and the true Church by imposing elements copied from Roman Catholicism's state church model upon the Protestant denominations they founded in Northern Europe. That was another major mistake, which, thankfully, the churches they founded had to leave behind in Europe when they immigrated to America, where state churches are, thank God, banned by the Constitution.

Though no one can deny that hyper-Calvinism is 100 percent consistent with Augustine's and John Calvin's teachings, it is something most Reformed churches have learned by experience to halt short of. I believe one reason is because vibrant evangelizing churches exist now in virtually every city and Reformists are well aware that presenting Calvinism too dogmatically may drive some adherents into the arms of the competition. Now that evangelical churches are beginning to flourish on Prince Edward Island, where I was born, I hear that even the Free Church of Scotland is amending its ways. Praise God for competition!

But why do so many logical people endorse a system of belief that by its very nature has to be kept on its meds?

A Few Psychological Observations

Anguish over the discomfiting fact that many of our fellow human beings, including some we love and have earnestly tried to persuade, will be lost forever, is an emotion every serious Christian seeks somehow to resolve. Already in *Heaven Wins*, we have found five ways people have of resolving that anguish:

1. Redefine hell as remedial, hence temporary—the Rob Bell solution.

2. God hasn't told us everything about it because it's not our concern—the Mark Galli solution, perhaps.

3. We all deserve hell anyway, so just be thankful at least some of us are saved—the Exclusivist solution.

4. Both election and reprobation are unconditional, so nothing is ultimately altered by what we choose or reject

let alone by what we do or don't do; and if you dare ask "why," you are setting yourself up as judging God—the reply some Calvinists offer.

5. No one will end up in heaven who is foreknown to reject every possible earthly persuasion to be God's friend; likewise, no one whose positive response to earthly persuasions is foreseen can be lost. If God foresees vital persuasions unavoidably blocked by the failure of others, God takes foreknown responders prior to their age of accountability, i.e., as children. This happens because potential response to foreknown earthly persuasions is just as real to a foreknowing God as is an actual response in real time. This is our *Heaven Wins* response.

As for the freewill minority who are lost because they choose to remain evil, they are the price God had to pay to own a very costly "pearl"—that blessed majority of once-fallen but now redeemed freewill-ers whose witness against evil in The Great Story enables God to create future hosts of freewill beings with 100 percent remaining faithful. With yet-to-exist "principalities and powers in heavenly places" thus persuaded, no further falls mar the future history of the cosmos. And that is how I personally solve the anguish I feel for the lost.

15

HOW CHRISTIANITY LOST ITS ORIGINAL ZEAL

In his insightful book *Cities of God,* Baylor University's remarkable historian, Rodney Stark, graphs the best historians' estimates of how many people in the Roman Empire had become Christians over intervals of time ranging from AD 40 to 350. Dr. Stark finds as follows: Peg Christianity's average rate of growth at 3.4 percent per year starting with a mere 1,000 believers in AD 40 and the total number of Christians soars to about 31.7 million people by AD 350. That number happened to approximate the consensus of several scholars that circa 50 percent of the inhabitants of the Empire professed to be Christians by then. And that was an increase achieved despite persecution and martyrdoms throughout![1]

Thus, by AD 350, if not earlier, Christians had completed their first truly major territorial accomplishment: the complete encirclement of the Mediterranean Sea with a 7,000-mile-long "church belt," an encompassing "lei" of more than 30 million Christians worshiping in tens of thousands of fellowships! This datum leads us to ask, what should Christians in that era have adopted as their *next* major goal?

Two Options

One option was simply to settle down and enjoy increasing prosperity under the largely persecution-free era Emperor Constantine had initiated. A second option was to exploit that conveniently handed-down, already-existing 7,000-mile-long "church belt"—purchased at the cost of inestimable labors, travail and martyrdoms—as a launching pad, a staging area, for a 360-degree outreach to the rest of the world!

Take fifth-century Saint Patrick as an example of what the Church as a whole could have achieved beyond the borders of the

Roman Empire in subsequent eras. Aided on the women's side of ministry by a remarkable Irish lady named Brigit, Patrick saw virtually an entire pagan society transformed by the power of the gospel within one man's and one woman's lifetime! Formerly pagan Irish, once evangelized—as Thomas Cahill has documented in *How the Irish Saved Civilization*[2]—contributed profoundly to mainland Europe in return.

Similarly evangelized, Vikings, Huns, Goths, Visigoths, Tartars, Vandals and Arabs could have become just-as-brotherly neighbors to a by then largely Christian Roman Empire. Left unevangelized by Christian bishops who had consigned the Great Commission to limbo, hordes of the above soon began pillaging Christian civilization and killing Christians. Unevangelized Arabs would even invent their own version of monotheism—Islam—and impose it by force over some 60 percent of what had been Christianity's primary domain.

And all the while the above threats were brewing, the east and west coasts of Africa, the North Sea and the Black Sea, the Nile and Volga Rivers, caravan routes across Asia and south into Arabia were all beckoning for Mediterranean Christianity to wake up and "do the work of evangelism."

Seafaring Vikings, about to pioneer sea lanes from Norway to Iceland to Greenland and even to the eastern tip of what is now Canada, would venture that far merely to explore; hunt deer, elk and moose; harvest pelts of fur and sail home. Imagine: Had they been transformed by the gospel, those same Vikings could have initiated the evangelization of the New World from the 600s onward!

Christians of Augustine's and Boniface's generation could have been mobilized to the task. What did Rodney Stark's 31 million mid-fourth century believers need to inspire them to spread the gospel abroad? All they needed was for the Church Fathers of that day to do what the apostles and their immediate successors had done during much of the prior three centuries: proclaim the Church as obligated to fulfill the Great Commission!

Instead, some Church Fathers began teaching exactly the opposite—that the Great Commission had been given only to the apostles, not to the Church. Other Church Fathers conveniently dropped the topic entirely. Read their letters, their treatises, their homilies, their liturgies, even their creeds, and reinforcement of

Christ's mandate to take the gospel to the ends of the earth is conspicuously absent. They mumble about "the Word of God in all the earth" as if it's somehow going to find its way to the ends of the earth on its own.

How dire was the consequence of their dilettante truncation of the apostolic message? Growth did not cease completely. At least a few Christians on the frontiers of the Empire kept trying to influence pagan neighbors. Sadly, what the Church Fathers of that blasé era sacrificed most tragically was the remarkably exponential nature of the earlier growth verified by Dr. Stark in *Cities of God*.

Yet, even Dr. Stark comments, "as the pool of potential recruits diminishes, at some point the rate of growth must slow down as well."[3] That, of course, would be true if the gospel was needed only by people within the Roman Empire but not needed by people elsewhere. Just to get things going, targeting northern Europe, Asia, Arabia and sub-Saharan Africa with cross-cultural evangelism and church planting would have replenished the Church's "pool of potential recruits" enormously.

But Stark is right in another way: Even with that degree of obedience, growth would have slowed, albeit because of two different factors: (1) the time it takes to reach distant regions, and (2) the time it takes to learn foreign languages upon arrival, evangelize and then stabilize former pagans as Christians who will reach out to still more distant regions. As one who has labored through that entire process, beginning with no published dictionary let alone a grammar or a bilingual instructor, I assure readers that it does take time.

To demonstrate how the Church settled for very much slower growth rates subsequent to AD 350, I will now adapt some of Rodney Stark's pre-AD 350 parameters that I may apply them to analyze the Church's post-AD 350 era.

1. I start by conservatively rounding Stark's approximation of 31,722,489 Christians down to an even 30 million as of a slightly later date, AD 366.

2. I also take Stark's pre-Constantine growth rate of 3.4 percent *per year* and reduce it drastically to a mere *20* percent

per generation for the post-Constantine era. I also define one generation as 33.3 years—the approximate span of years in which a person is mature enough to use language persuasively, given the shorter life spans of people who lived long ago. This span of time (33.3 years) also fits handily as three generations per century.

What, then, does a 20 percent per generation growth rate require of, let's say, a typical group of five post-Constantine Christians? First of all, each of the five must replace himself or herself with another stable Christian before he or she dies. Their replacements can of course be from among their own children, which one might consider the handiest method of spiritual replacement. *In addition, at least one of the five, or perhaps all five together, must somehow persuade just one more person to acknowledge Jesus Christ as his or her Lord and Savior.* Again, that sixth person can even be another child of one of the five. And how much time do all five Christians have to replace themselves with five new believers plus win just one more convert between them?

The correct answer is: 33.3 years!

Surely we can all agree that reasonably motivated Post-Constantine Christians should have been able to sustain a growth rate as extremely minimal as 20 percent *per generation* (which is less than 0.6 percent per year) from AD 350 onward. Even if they simply raised their own children to love the Lord while making *zero* effort to evangelize distant pagans or anyone else, there should have been no problem.

Now, taking AD 366 as a starting point, we calculate a 20 percent growth rate per generation as follows, deleting decimal portions of years in column one:

Projected Increase in # of Christians

Year AD	Approximate # of Christians
366	30 million
400	36 million
433	43.2 million

466	51.84 million
500	62.21 million
533	74.65 million
566	89.58 million
600	107.50 million
633	128.99 million
666	154.79 million
700	185.75 million
733	222.90 million
766	267.48 million
800	320.98 million
833	385.18 million
866	462.21 million
900	554.65 million
933	665.58 million
966	798.70 million
1000	958.44 million
1033	1.15 billion
1066	1.38 billion
1100	1.656 billion
1133	1.987 billion
1166	2.385 billion

What a tragic surprise! By the end of a mere eight centuries after AD 366, even with a plodding growth rate of 20 percent per generation (which, again, is much less than Stark's estimate of 3.4 percent per year), the number of Christians on earth would have *exceeded* by far the total number alive in this twenty-first century.

According to a late 2011 report by The Pew Forum on Religion and Public Life, a demographic study of over 200 countries finds 2.18 billion Christians of all kinds and ages worldwide—nearly quadruple the figure of 100 years ago.[4]

This utterly shocking contrast between Rodney Stark's 3.4 percent *per year* increase from year 40 to year 350, and Christianity's calamitous post-AD 350 plunge—apparently even to levels of *negative* growth—clamors to be explained. Something was going horribly, tragically, disobediently and shamefully wrong that we dare not excuse with pathetic milquetoast references to "divine election not wanting anything more."

Obviously, Christian parents were failing in large measure even to replace themselves from among their own children, let alone to evangelize non-Christians. What was happening? I offer the following sample of inherent problems:

1. Beginning at least with Augustine, standards of Christ-like leadership were falling. The more prelates saw themselves as tenured by each other and supported by the Roman state, the less they saw themselves as answerable to God and to their congregants.

2. Merely living near a church could qualify you to be baptized and join the congregation. Evidence of newness of life in Christ no longer mattered prior to being baptized and partaking of the Lord's Supper. As more and more bishops simply assimilated huge numbers of unbelievers as church members, primarily just to gain some measure of control over them and then benefit from them, genuine evangelism became a museum artifact.

3. Parents, assured that infant baptism by a priest effectively secured their children's salvation, became not only less concerned but also less adept at leading their own children to repentance and faith, even if the parents themselves were genuine believers.

4. Other church leaders tried to shame their less godly peers by resorting to more and more extreme degrees of asceticism—not the wisest or most persuasive response by a long shot!

5. Though many zealous young Christians no doubt were eager to serve Christ, when they sought guidance as to how Christ was to be served, bishops failed to direct them to evangelize abroad. Cross-cultural mission was

no longer seen as incumbent on the Church. Paul's example in sending Timothy, Titus, Epaphroditus and Silas to evangelize a variety of faraway pagan areas was barely emulated.

Instead, some prelates urged already devout men to seek still higher levels of personal holiness by becoming hermits in caves or—as did Chrysostom himself—perching atop pillars like utter fools. Perfecting one's own "holiness" was deemed better than guiding the lost to redemption, as if both goals could not be pursued simultaneously. Increasingly, the Church substituted abject asceticism for resolute obedience to the Lord's Great Commission.

6. The Great Commission was not only de-commissioned but even revoked by prelates who taught that Jesus gave it not to his Church but only to the Apostles. As for Augustine, he did not even have to say what he thought about the Great Commission. Merely by defining human depravity as total, the election of lost people as unconditionally guaranteed by God himself and God's grace as irresistibly at work apart from human endeavor, Augustine effectively persuaded most Christians that evangelism was an exercise in futility. Thus he made himself a greater menace to the Church than the Manichæanism he had earlier espoused and later abandoned.

Why bother evangelizing? Let God's grace irresistibly secure what God's unconditional election has already set in place from eternity anyway. Trying to help God do what only God can do was deemed pridefully insulting to God.

Thus, by the fifth century much of the Mediterranean-area Church resembled that stagnant, evangelism-less Free Church of Scotland in early nineteenth-century Argyle Shore, Prince Edward Island. Augustine—by forcibly preserving the Church as a monolith and teaching Christians to misread passages such as Romans 8:29

and Ephesians 2:1—contributed to debilitating the Church founded by Jesus and his apostles into a self-satisfied, virtually no-growth entity the apostles would have had difficulty recognizing as a church. Roman Catholicism was birthing.

Little wonder the Lord said (no doubt with a sigh) what Luke 18:8 records:

When the Son of Man comes, will he find faith on the earth?

Yet he is the One who keeps finding ways to help us rebuild what has crumbled, even if we keep misusing or breaking the tools he provides.

In a day when some Romans were accusing Christianity of weakening the Roman Empire's ability to resist barbarian invasions, Augustine countered by writing a book titled *The City of God*. In it, Augustine responded by demonstrating positive ways in which Christians had improved the quality of Roman life.

One wonders: Did it occur to Augustine that if only the Great Commission had been kept on the cutting edge of Christian thought in the prior century, many of those very barbarians would already be Christian neighbors too busy spreading the gospel farther afield to even think of invading the empire that gave them the gospel?

Even the very title *City of God* forewarns of Augustine's unabashed preference for merging Christianity and the political power of the Roman state together—a union he apparently thought would enhance the church.

INCOMPLETE CREEDS AS SYMPTOMATIC WARNINGS

Historians are unsure who first penned the Apostles' Creed or when, yet most of its primary components are found in Chrysostom's Liturgy, dated perhaps as early as the 380s. The following reads like an echo of an already existing Apostles' Creed if not a prototype for the original:

> Having in remembrance, therefore, this saving command-
> ment and all those things which have come to pass for us:
> the Cross, the Grave, the Resurrection on the third day, the
> Ascension into heaven, the Sitting at the right hand, and the
> second and glorious Coming.[1]

As a child of 11 years, like hundreds of millions of Christians over the last 17 or so centuries, I memorized the Apostles' Creed and have quoted it hundreds of times in church services, especially in my youth. Hearing it sung by a choir filled me with awe. Then came the day when I realized with sorrow that whoever formulated and approved the Apostles' Creed endorsed the omission of something that was extremely important to the apostles.

Whether it is Chrysostom's liturgy above, the full version of the Apostle's Creed or even the Nicene Creed, the same crucial component is deleted. Midway through each such attestation, we affirm belief in our Lord's resurrection and his ascension into heaven, thereby implying that nothing worthy of mention happened *between* these two major events!

Jesus did not rise from the dead and ascend to heaven on the same day, nor in the same week, nor even in the same *month*! A span of 40 days intervened during which he gave a command as important for all of us as are the resurrection and the ascension both! It was also a command many Church Fathers by the time of Chrysostom were ignoring to their shame—a command apart from which the churches they were administering would not even exist!

The men we call "Church Fathers" were either conspiring or consenting to delete our Lord's *Great Commission* from the teaching agenda of the Church.

The Beginning of the *Great Omission*

The decision to omit the Great Commission from the Creeds begat numerous tragic after-effects. For example, the various Creeds served as "templates" encouraging the development of increasingly systematized theology. Inevitably, mission-less templates began begetting mission-less theology. How tragic!

In my self-published tome *Unhidden*, available only from my website (www.donrichardsonbooksales.com), I call for a new sentence to be installed at last in the Creeds. Following the words "On the third day He rose again from the dead," insert this:

> He commissioned his Church, beginning with the Apostles,
> to proclaim repentance and forgiveness of sins to all nations.

I treasure a Sunday bulletin from a church where I spoke recently. It has the Great Commission as worded above added to the Apostles' Creed, ready to be read by the congregation. The insert is followed by, "After that, he ascended into heaven" and the rest of the Creed as typically recited. Surely, if the Church Fathers we honor in our hymnology had deigned to include one such simple statement acknowledging our Lord as commissioning his Church to evangelize the world, history's subsequent abysmal narrative would have been significantly upgraded.

Keep in mind that the Church Fathers' mission-less Creeds served as "pocket Bibles" for millions of Christians who had no access to Scripture. Mission-less Creeds thus misrepresented the Bible by telling Christians many wonderful truths to believe but saying absolutely nothing regarding what God might want them to do to advance his kingdom!

How many sermons would have been preached about the Great Commission if preachers looking for a topic had found it mentioned in something as noteworthy as a Creed? If even a small percentage of hundreds of millions of memorizers were inspired to action by one added phrase about the Great Commission, who knows how many might have ventured forth among Vikings, Goths, Visigoths, Tartars, Vandals, Arabs, Hindus and tribes in sub-Saharan Africa. Try to imagine how much blessing a few extra words might have generated. Consider the following examples.

In 1268, Nikolo and Matteo Polo arrived in Rome bearing a request from Kublai Khan, grandson of Genghis Khan, for 100 scholars to teach Christianity and science to the entire Mongol Nation. Hapless Pope Gregory X sent only two friars, both of whom turned back mid-journey.

If Pope Gregory, who may have cared little for Scripture, at least had found the Great Commission in a Creed he was appointed to uphold, perhaps he would have done more to arrange for Kublai Khan and immense throngs of Mongols and Chinese to receive the gospel of Jesus instead of converting to Buddhism! New churches could then have been planted across China and Mongolia beginning almost six centuries before Robert Morrison, Hudson Taylor and others began preaching in China in the 1800s. And, Chinese who embraced the gospel might have also prevented Islam from closing the Silk Road and limiting European access to Southeast Asia by the sea.[2]

Late in the 1700s, William Carey, an English cobbler, urged a group of pastors conferring in Nottingham, England, to respond to the Great Commission by forming a society to begin sending missionaries abroad to "the heathen." A certain pastor, J. C. Ryland, was said to promptly stand up and impatiently interrupt William Carey with, "Sit down, young man, sit down and be still. When God wants to convert the heathen, He will do it without consulting either you or me."[3]

Unaware how besotted he was by misleading suppositions on divine sovereignty traceable via Calvin all the way back to Augustine, Ryland could easily voice so unspeakable an error with a clear conscience. Later, thank God, reading a little book by William Carey (referred to in footnote 8 of chapter 11) helped to fill in for Ryland what the Creeds left out. Ryland changed his mind and began supporting Carey.

No matter how many books impassioned John Piper writes advocating Reformed theology as the finest-ever stimulant for world missions, I remain impressed by John Piper but not by his Calvinism. The missionaries Piper cites as if they were inspired by Calvinist doctrine alone also had the prior example of the apostles, and many undoubtedly knew of earlier non-Reformist missionaries like the Moravians. The latter went abroad with the gospel from the 1730s onward. Real-life examples probably played their part as well.

The many brave Lutheran missionaries who in later centuries ventured courageously beyond Europe to evangelize people like the Santal in India and the cannibal Batak in northern Sumatra also had the same real-life examples for their inspiration.

History itself reveals Augustine's personal indifference to the spiritual need of lands beyond the Roman Empire. Looking back to the time of the Reformation, historian Gustav Warneck (in company with others) provides a wealth of quotations from the personal letters of virtually every Reformer as to how each one perceived the Church's duty to spread the gospel beyond Protestant Europe. Virtually every quotation excuses the Church of all responsibility. Read them and weep, or at least sigh. Here is an example from John Calvin himself:

> We are taught [from Scripture] that the kingdom of Christ is neither to be advanced nor maintained by the industry of men, but this is the work of God alone.[4]

Come again? What about marching orders already given by our Lord himself, and only partially obeyed? Following this quotation from Calvin, Warneck *et al.* offer their own further comments:

> Hence for him also [Calvin] it follows necessarily that a special institution for the extension of Christianity among non-Christian nations, i.e., for missions, is needless. . . . It may also be noticed that Calvin's exposition of the

missionary commandment is silent regarding a missionary duty on the part of the Church. . . . the command to go into all the world is spoken of [by Calvin] only in regard to the Apostles, not indeed in such a way as to exclude its application to subsequent generations, but yet without any such application.[5]

Still, though John Calvin and his colleagues in Geneva were mainly concerned to spread the gospel to other parts of Europe, there was one minuscule exception. One of Calvin's acquaintances in Geneva received a letter from a friend in Brazil requesting a team of preachers to bring the gospel to a northeastern part of that nation. In response, 14 people ventured across the Atlantic. Some met with disaster and others soon abandoned the mission. The whole enterprise ended as little more than a short-term stint.

As for Martin Luther himself, a certain Lutheran historian, challenged to prove that Martin Luther manifested a clear concern for the non-Christian world, perused Luther's many papers to find only one plausible quotation. Learning that Christian soldiers had been captured by Muslim Turks in Eastern Europe, Luther wrote that those Christian soldiers should conduct themselves so as hopefully to lead their Muslim captors to Christ.[6]

Bravo, Luther! Soldiers setting forth with swords make a fine substitute for language-learning missionaries bearing Scripture and the gospel. To a man, the Classical Reformers had no problem accepting mission-less Creeds handed down from that era when the initial expansion documented by Rodney Stark was ending and the great growth dearth began.

Again and again, when the Classical Reformers refer in their writings to the Word of God spreading "into all the earth," it's mainly as if God's Word is to get there by its own means or by some post-millennial apocalyptic miracle. That the Church is commissioned to preach the gospel to the ends of the earth until the end of this present age gets overlooked.

That said, other branches of conservative theology also have a problem keeping the Great Commission in sight. A professor of missions on a certain evangelical seminary campus once remarked to me, "The school of theology and the school of missions on this campus are connected only by the plumbing."

The Great Commission, a Shocking Surprise!

For Jewish rabbis two millennia ago, a Messiah who commissioned Jews to preach repentance and forgiveness of sins to every Gentile nation was totally unwelcome. Preoccupied primarily with Israel's *political* destiny, rabbis anticipated Israel's Messiah coming to provide not salvation from sin but *political deliverance* for Israel. They taught that Messiah must lead a Jewish army to victory over Rome, Israel's oppressor. The Son of David must replace Caesar as world ruler. Jerusalem must replace Rome as the capital city of the world!

That is why the Jewish people (Jesus' disciples included) were left with no warning outside of Scripture itself that Israel's Messiah must come initially to *suffer, die and rise from the dead*, thus becoming the Lamb of God who takes away the sin of the world. That is also why Jesus' disciples, raised under that rabbinic influence, saw their Master's crucifixion and death as incompatible with the role of Messiah as a political emancipator, a societal deliverer.

When two of them, on their way to Emmaus, admitted, "We had hoped that he was the one who was going to redeem Israel" (Luke 24:21), they were referring not to Jesus redeeming Israel from *sin* but from Roman oppression. How could a crucified *victim* be the regal *victor* everyone was anticipating? Though Jesus often spoke of freeing people from sin, surely freeing Israel from Rome was primary, wasn't it?

Even Peter, confused and dispirited, thought his only option after the crucifixion was to go back to fishing for fish, not men. None of the disciples had the slightest inkling that Jesus' demise meant salvation for mankind. How then did Jesus, risen from the dead, set his disciples straight about God's unfolding purpose?

The Deep Teaching Our Lord Saved Till the Last

In the final chapter of his Gospel, Luke reveals that Jesus, during that 40-day span, "opened [his disciples'] minds" (see Luke 24:45) to comprehend two very profound Old Testament themes. Let me call them Mega Theme "A" and Mega Theme "B." These were themes stretching throughout Old Testament Scripture from Genesis to Malachi, themes that for centuries remained conspicuously overlooked by Jewish rabbis. At last, via one poignantly convincing twin-track discourse, Jesus would enable his disciples to understand why that dreadful event—the crucifixion—had to happen, only to be followed by the resurrection. They would also understand what must happen next as a logical follow-through to both the crucifixion and the resurrection.

In his three years of public ministry, Jesus had "micro-taught" a wide selection of brief Old Testament texts. Now the risen Lord was teaching his disciples again, but with a mega difference! Rather than briefly exposit a few more disconnected texts, we find Jesus presenting a comprehensive survey of key Old Testament Scriptures as he taught two disciples on the road to Emmaus:

> And beginning with Moses and all the Prophets, he explained to them what was said in *all the Scriptures* concerning himself (Luke 24:27).

Again, later, amid the larger group of his disciples in Jerusalem, perhaps even in the same upper room where they had celebrated Passover together before his death, Jesus "opened their minds so they could understand the Scriptures" (v. 45)—Scriptures his disciples probably thought they already knew quite well.

The first major theme Jesus enabled his disciples to grasp on these two occasions was one so profoundly all-encompassing that it must have filled them with awe. But it also prepared them for something more—to be led atop the Mount of Olives and be given the Great Commission later! These are what I call Mega Theme "A" and Mega Theme "B."

Mega Theme "A":
The Messiah Who Suffers, Dies and Rises

To introduce Mega Theme A, Jesus said:

> This is what is written: The Christ will suffer and rise from the dead on the third day (Luke 24:46).

As he had done for the two disciples on the way to Emmaus, again in Jerusalem Jesus led a larger group of his disciples through what to them must have seemed like a maze of Old Testament prophecies. Imagine Jesus, for a start, expositing Genesis 3:15, where God, following the fall of mankind, warned the Serpent:

> I will put enmity between you and the woman, and between your offspring and *hers*.

All through the Old Testament it was culturally appropriate to credit the male parent for an offspring. Abraham, for example, is known as "son of Terah" (Genesis 11:26). Who, then, was Abraham's mother? We do not know the name of that important woman. Even when the name of a mother was known, she was rarely mentioned as a matter of historical reference. But God, in Genesis 3:15, is speaking of someone who was to be born of a *woman*, with no human male parent to be credited as his father! God continued:

> He will crush your head and you will strike his heel.

Israel anticipated a societal deliverer who would crush the head of a temporal despot, a merely human enemy—a Caesar, for example. Jesus identified the one whose head Messiah would crush as mankind's ultimate enemy—the Serpent.

Imagine Jesus identifying himself as the Seed of the woman whose heel was struck while in the process of crushing the serpent's head. Hear him quoting also other prophecies fulfilled by his recent suffering on Golgotha:

> They have pierced my hands and my feet. . . . They divide my garments among them and cast lots for my clothing (Psalm 22:16,18).

> He was pierced for our transgressions, he was crushed for our iniquities; the punishment that brought us peace was upon him and, by his wounds we are healed. We all, like sheep, have gone astray, each of us has turned to his

own way; and the LORD has laid on him the iniquity of us all. . . . He was assigned a grave with the wicked, and with the rich in his death, though he had done no violence, nor was any deceit in his mouth (Isaiah 53:5-6,9).

You will not abandon me to the grave nor let your Holy One see decay (Psalm 16:10).

Jesus' disciples suddenly realized that these and many other prophecies he was citing were all fulfilled there and then before their very eyes. How intense the awe that must have overwhelmed them!

What Abraham Foreshadowed in the Region of Moriah

Imagine Jesus explaining why, two millennia earlier (see Genesis 22:1-12), God ordered the near sacrifice of Abraham's son Isaac to happen, not on Mount Moriah itself nor just anywhere Abraham might choose in that general area, but specifically, "on one of the mountains I will tell you about" *near* Moriah. According to long-ago Jewish historian Josephus, Mount Moriah is the Temple Mount, and the adjacent "region of Moriah" is where the old walled city of Jerusalem would later stand.

Why did Abraham's incredible test of obedience have to be linked to so precise a location—a "spot X," if you will? Genesis 22:5 reveals that Abraham, instead of loading on the donkey the firewood on which his beloved son of promise was to be offered, left the donkey behind with two servants. That strange choice ordained Isaac to be the one who must struggle up the final slope bearing the wood on which he was to be offered by his anguished but resolute father. What a precise foreshadowing of Jesus—a greater Isaac—carrying another load of wood in the shape of a Roman cross to the summit of Calvary, a mountain, no less, *adjacent* to Mount Moriah.

On that occasion centuries later, no ram was found to take the greater Isaac's place. God, the greater Father, completed the necessary sacrifice of a beloved only Son, which of course he never intended Abraham, a mere human father, to complete 2,000 years before. Thus did God give Abraham the inestimable privilege of presenting mankind with so precise a foreshadowing of what would later happen, and even *where*! How fittingly Abraham decided to name the mountain God had specified, "The LORD Will Provide" (Genesis 22:14).

With their minds thus opened to grasp Mega Theme A, Jesus' disciples at last perceived their Lord as the One who, from before creation, was destined to offer himself as a sacrifice before ascending on high as Savior and Sovereign.

But Mega Theme A was not the whole message. A complete impartation of what was to be the primary apostolic teaching agenda required Jesus to open his disciples' minds *again*—this time to impart what I call Mega Theme B.

Mega Theme "B": The Great Commission in the Old Testament

Unless Jesus' disciples grasped the Great Commission as a necessary corollary to his crucifixion and resurrection, they would hardly be ready to obey it. Whereas Mega Theme A enabled Jesus' disciples to grasp Old Testament Scripture in ways that were typically beyond the ken of Jewish rabbis, only Mega Theme B could convince the disciples that Mega Theme A's profound message must be offered to Gentiles as well as to their fellow Jews. Luke 24:47 shows how Jesus continued:

> And repentance and forgiveness of sins will be preached in his name to all nations, beginning at Jerusalem [but by no means ending there].

Where could Jesus find that kind of teaching in the Old Testament Scriptures (which is all he had from which to draw support)? To "unseal" the grandeur of his Mega Theme B, Jesus had only to highlight an intensely missional five-times-repeated, even oath-sealed promise featured in the Bible's first book, Genesis. Shattering a stereotype that views God in the Old Testament as coddling Israel and ignoring Gentiles, Jesus no doubt offered his disciples quote after quote filled with promises of blessing for *Gentiles*.

For Abraham, the Same Promise
Given Three Times and Oath-Sealed!

Ratifying a covenant with a Chaldean named Abraham (father of nations), God promised to bless the man himself even to the extent of founding a new nation through him. Yet God added also another purpose:

> All peoples on earth will be blessed through you (Genesis 12:3).

Abraham thus found himself enfranchised, so to speak, to disseminate a blessing originating in God and targeted, not just for the Hebrews, but for "all peoples on earth."

Again, on the eve of the destruction of Sodom and Gomorrah, God articulated both parts of the same covenant a second time:

> Abraham will surely become a great and powerful nation, and all nations on earth will be blessed through him (Genesis 18:18).

God's reminder had the desired effect. Abraham responded by stepping into a role that was new for him. Negotiating with God as a newly appointed "blessor" for Gentiles, Abraham negotiated a basis whereby mercy might preempt judgment—not just for his Hebrew nephew Lot and his family but for all the Gentile people in Sodom and Gomorrah as well. Indeed, both cities would have been spared had they measured up to the minimal requirement Abraham had negotiated for their deliverance.

Later, responding to Abraham's willingness to place Isaac on that altar in the region of Moriah, God affirmed the same covenant again, but this third time God added a powerful emphasis by sealing his promises with his own personal oath, saying:

> *I swear by myself* . . . that because you have done this and have not withheld your son, your only son, I will surely bless you and make your descendants as numerous as the stars in the sky and as the sand on the seashore. Your descendants will take possession of the cities of their enemies (Genesis 22:16-17).

God then also affirmed the latter part of his covenant, adding, "and through your offspring all nations on earth will be blessed, because you have obeyed me" (v. 18). Thus, by his own choice, God bound himself by an oath to bless all peoples on earth through Abraham and his descendants. To the degree that we find it unthinkable that God would make himself guilty of perjury, we should find it equally unthinkable that he would allow the history of this planet to culminate with his oath-sealed promise unfulfilled.

For Isaac, the Same Promise a *Fourth* Time

Isaac, Abraham's son conceived in response to a test of faith, was the next patriarch to hear God assure blessing for him, followed by a promise:

> Through your offspring all nations on earth will be blessed (Genesis 26:4).

For Jacob, the Same Promise a *Fifth* Time

For Abraham's grandson Jacob, God amplified his promise again in Genesis 28:14:

> Your descendants will be like the dust of the earth, and you will spread out to the west and to the east, to the north and to the south. All peoples on earth will be blessed through you and your offspring.

God's reason for promising to disperse large numbers of the patriarchal progeny to the four coordinates of the earth was not for military conquest, financial gain or resettlement but simply to "bless all peoples on earth"! God was announcing a time when he would arrange for Abraham, Isaac and Jacob's progeny to be uprooted as necessary so as to be scattered as blessing-bearers far out into Gentile realms.

God's again-and-again repeated oath-sealed intention to disperse Abraham's descendants like dust to bless all peoples on earth signifies nothing less than the New Testament's Great Commission emerging in its Old Testament prototype. So—did the *diaspora* (dispersion) promised in Genesis 28:14 actually happen? It did indeed! For example, Genesis—Moses' first book—culminates with Joseph being snatched away into Egypt to become a blessing for Egyptians as well as his fellow Hebrews, resulting in all of the Hebrews immigrating to Egypt.

Joseph thus becomes the model blessor for Gentiles! Failure to emulate the Joseph standard would ever be to live below the ideal of God's missional covenant. Also, by whom was much of the Old Testament written? By deported or about-to-be-deported Israelites who, as a result of being deported, were destined to bless Gentiles in divinely ordained ways.

How, then, did subsequent generations fare or falter in relation to that remarkable "Joseph standard"? Let's look at the list a little closer.

How the Genesis 28:14 "Dust" Began Spreading Multi-Culturally

Hebrew Person:	To Whom Sent:	Went Because:	Result:
Abraham and Sarah	Egyptians	Ousted by a famine	Deported from Egypt
Abraham	Melchizedek	Wanted to bless	Paid a tithe
Abraham and Sarah	A Philistine king	Ousted by a famine	Mixed result
Joseph	Egyptians	Sold as a slave	Blessed all of Egypt
Moses	Jethro, a Midianite	Fled from Egypt	Jethro came to faith
Joshua and the spies	Rahab, a Canaanite	She hid the spies	Rahab came to faith
Naomi	Ruth, a Moabite	Ousted by a famine	Ruth came to faith
David	Gibeonites	Justice required	Peace restored
Elijah	A Canaanite widow	Needed refuge	Her son resurrected
Hebrew girl	Naaman, a Syrian	Taken as a slave	Naaman healed
Elisha	Damascus	Honored as a hero	2 Kings 6:18-23; 8:7
Jonah	People of Nineveh	Called by God	Nineveh repented
Daniel and friends	Babylonians	Mass deportation	Babylonians blessed

Some biblical scholars claim that Jews, far from being commissioned to go out on missions of blessing to Gentile nations, were supposed to simply stay at home, hoping Gentiles would visit Israel and be blessed. Visitors indeed were to be welcomed, but that was not God's sole intention.

As evidence, note how two New Testament apostles identify Jesus and the spread of the gospel as fulfilling exactly what Genesis had emphasized. Acts 3:25 records Peter—with Jesus' mind-opening post-resurrection discourse still fresh in his memory—reminding the Jews of what God had long before said to Abraham:

Through your offspring all peoples on earth will be blessed.

Signifying what? Peter explains:

When God raised up his servant [Jesus as Messiah], he sent him first to you to bless you by turning each of you from your wicked ways (v. 26).

Peter's "first to you to bless you" implies "*second* to bless Gentiles" by virtue of fulfilling the Great Commission. Paul makes the same connection even more specifically in Galatians 3:6 and 8:

Consider Abraham: "He believed God, and it was credited to him as righteousness". . . . Scripture foresaw that God would justify the Gentiles by faith and announced the gospel in advance to Abraham: "All nations will be blessed through you."

Please note: What I described in chapter 9 as "a *pentalogue*" found in Genesis has now become a "*septalogue*" with the addition of the above two quotes found in the New Testament. Note also how inextricably Peter and Paul link "the New Testament gospel" with God's Old Testament promise of blessing for Gentiles worldwide. Paul even went on to affirm Gentile believers as Abraham's spiritual descendants! In Galatians 3:29, Paul assured Gentile Christians in Galatia:

If you belong to Christ, then you are Abraham's seed, and heirs according to the promise.

Thus, all of us who believe in Jesus as Abraham's true "seed" are viewed by God as spiritually descended from Abraham. This means that we too participate in God's worldwide mission by joining in the task of blessing all peoples on earth in God's very special ordained way.

Note that the final clause in all five passages proffers a divinely appointed "franchise" for Abraham and his progeny by saying, "All peoples on earth will be blessed *through you*" or "through you *and your descendants*." God did not commission a task force of holy angels for this unique and eternally momentous task. Assigning this incredible mission to angels who have never known evil would undercut the poignancy of The Great Story postulated earlier in chapter 1. Instead he commissioned Abraham and his spiritual progeny to serve as blessors for Gentile blessees worldwide. Abraham's spiritual progeny—the Church—thus possesses what can best be termed a "blessor franchise." But what has the Church done with it?

One would think that—since God gave that promise five times to three Hebrew patriarchs and even confirmed it with his own personal oath!—rabbis would teach such a strongly emphasized promise to Jewish boys preparing for their bar mitzvahs. Not so. Jewish friends who are now Christians assure me that rabbis nonchalantly relegate the mission God entrusted to Israel to the shadows.

But this is only a beginning; a promise of blessing for Abraham and/or Israel linked with a promise of blessing for Gentiles is paraphrased in more than 200 other passages in the Bible. The examples on page 202 illustrate these promises.

Clearly, when Jesus opened his disciples' minds to understand Mega Theme A, not alone but in conjunction with Mega Theme B, he intended *both* themes to be kept linked as the primary teaching agenda both for the apostles and for the Church. Keeping both themes linked is what inspired the incredibly rapid wholesale expansion of the Early Church into such a variety of linguistic and cultural settings, as documented by Rodney Stark. But by Augustine's day, Christian

Paraphrases of the Abrahamic Covenant

Reference	Blessing for Abraham and His Progeny	Blessing for Gentiles
Psalm 47:4,9	"He chose our inheritance for us."	"The nobles of the nations assemble as the people of the God of Abraham."
Psalm 67:1-2	"God be gracious to us . . ."	"that your ways may be known on earth, your salvation among all nations."
Psalm 67:7	"God will bless us . . ."	"and all the ends of the earth will fear him."
Psalm 72:17	"And they will call him blessed."	"All nations will be blessed through him."
Psalm 87:2,4,6	"The Lord loves the gates of Zion."	"I will record Rahab and Babylon among those who acknowledge me—Philistia too, and Tyre, along with Cush. . . . The Lord will write in the register of the peoples: 'This one [a Gentile] was born in Zion.'"
Psalm 98:2-3	"He has remembered his love and his faithfulness to . . . Israel."	"The Lord has made his salvation known and revealed his righteousness to the nations."
Isaiah 26:12,18	"Lord, you establish peace for us."	"We have not brought salvation to the earth; [nor] given birth to people of the world."
Acts 26:23	"Christ would suffer and, as the first to rise from the dead, would proclaim light to his own people . . ."	"and to the Gentiles."
Romans 15:8-9	"Christ has become a servant of the Jews . . . to confirm the promises made to the Patriarchs . . ."	"so that the Gentiles may glorify God for his mercy."
Galatians 3:14	"[Christ] redeemed us in order that the blessing given to Abraham . . ."	"might come to the Gentiles through Christ Jesus."
Acts 28:23,28	"From morning till evening [Paul] . . . declared [to the Jews in Rome] the kingdom of God."	"Therefore . . . know that God's salvation has been sent to the Gentiles, and they will listen."

Church Fathers had halved our Lord's primary teaching agenda by relegating Mega Theme B to the dustbin just as Jewish rabbis had done and still do in favor of other agendas.

Augustine said nothing to bring Theme A and Theme B together again, hence the stark contrast between the health of the pre-Augustine Church and the anemia of the Church in subsequent eras.

What of modern Christian theologians? As Gentiles themselves, surely they will grasp the import of a five-times-given, sealed-by-divine-oath promise of blessing for Gentiles. Surely they would also recognize that the "All peoples on earth will be blessed through you" promise is quoted twice and paraphrased a dozen times in the New Testament in addition to the five occurrences in Genesis. Wouldn't they at least assign that blessed concept an honorific title from Greek or Latin, as they do for other aspects of Scripture (Pentateuch, Decalogue, *diaspora*, *imago Dei*, and so on)?

Alas, modern Christian theologians have been until recently almost as remiss as the later Church Fathers and Jewish rabbis. How contentedly they too have left a promise given five times to three patriarchs—a promise sealed under divine oath—bereft of even an honorific title from a classical language, let alone extensive commentary.

No matter! Better late than never! If the Ten Commandments can be called "the Decalogue," let us here and now affirm God's five-times-given promise of blessing for all peoples on Earth as his "*Pentalogue*"!

That same Great Commission would later be echoed by Isaiah's "Whom shall I send? And who will go for us?" (Isaiah 6:8) and "Go, swift messengers" (Isaiah 18:2). Old Testament Scripture shows the blessor franchise fulfilled by relatively few—Joseph, Naomi, Elijah, Elisha, Jeremiah, Ezekiel, Daniel and others like them who reached out to Gentiles and blessed them profoundly. Are not they the ones most favored to have their biographies featured prominently in the canon of Scripture?

Why the Great Commission Was
Definitely Not to Be Deleted

One of the most pointed parables our Lord taught was his Parable of
the Tenant Farmers in Matthew 21:33-43, which can be interpreted
as follows.

A landowner (God) planted a vineyard—this world filled with
people God designed to be "reaped" as citizens for his kingdom. He
rented his vineyard to tenant farmers who of course were entitled to
keep some of the fruit of the vineyard for themselves—Abrahamic
blessing for Israel! The remainder of the produce—i.e., Gentiles who
were recipients of Genesis 12:3 to 28:14 blessing as a result of their
management of God's "property"—was to be for the Owner.

Time and again, despite successive pleas, the tenant farmers
denied the Owner what was rightfully his. Jesus was designating the
large majority of Jews who refused to teach significant numbers of
Gentiles to believe in the one true God. Spurning multiple warnings,
the tenants even eventually killed the Owner's son. So also the Jews,
after persecuting many Old Testament prophets, also delivered Jesus
to be crucified. End result: The Owner transferred the privilege of
managing his vineyard to "other tenants, who would give him his
share of the crop at harvest time" (Matthew 21:41).

Jesus thus pointedly attested that Israel had exhausted God's
patience. He would no longer employ Israel as his primary means of
blessing "all peoples on earth" by harvesting, as Revelation 7:9 puts it:

A great multitude . . . from every nation, tribe, people, and
language.

That inestimable privilege has now been transferred to the
predominantly Gentile Christian Church. And God expects the
Church not to repeat Israel's mismanagement of his vineyard. A
second era of mismanagement will constitute an intolerable insult
to a very patient, very gracious vineyard Owner! That is why, by
deleting the Great Commission from our Creeds and from the
Church's teaching agenda, Augustine and many other fourth-
century so-called bishops were walking ingloriously backward
in time!

We are not here to loll and frolic but to bring in a harvest for God. Recall Jeremiah 2:3, quoted earlier:

> Israel was holy to the LORD, the firstfruits of his harvest.

Designating a relatively small number of Israelite believers as only the *firstfruits* is God's way of letting us know that He also anticipates a massively greater *harvest* from across the vast reaches of the Gentile world. That is the task assigned. Are we up to it?

God's Mission, from Israel to the Church, and then Back—to Israel?

In Romans 11:25, Paul references Israel's past failure parabled above with a warning to the Church:

> I do not want you to be ignorant of this mystery, brothers.

Paul is referring to God's fivefold, oath-sealed promise to Abraham, Isaac and Jacob. God is still determined to bless "all peoples on earth" via a select group of blessors—if not by Israel formerly, at last by the Church laterally, as in *now*! By leaving God's powerfully emphasized mission untaught, rabbis had consigned it to a "mystery bin," provoking God to transfer it over for the Church to finish.

Paul's concern is that the Church, growing conceited by finding it has moved to "downtown central" in God's purpose, may lose sight of what it is to do. But Paul then adds an encouragingly hopeful promise, saying:

> Israel has experienced a hardening in part [by saying "Yes" to the law, "Yes" to the Sabbath, "Yes" to keeping dairy and meat products separate for kosher purposes, but "NO!" to that oath-sealed Abrahamic mission] until . . .

Until what? Paul is letting us know that something will eventually cause the Jews to want God to give his mission back to them. What could that be? Paul explains what it will take:

> Until the full number of the Gentiles has come in. And so all
> Israel will be saved (Romans 11:25-26).

Note the chronology here. First Israel provides the firstfruits, whereupon the Church completes the *harvest* by bringing in at least some (we try for many, of course) to faith from every tribe, people, nation and language. But why then would the Jews want to wrest an already completed mission back from the Church? Oh, I think I see why! As Jesus forewarned:

> Not the smallest letter nor the least stroke of a pen will
> by any means disappear from the Law until everything is
> accomplished (Matthew 5:18).

God's requirement that every key aspect of the law must be fulfilled thus assures that a firstfruits phase and a harvest phase must presage a *gleaning* phase to follow!

Once the Church completes God's harvest by bringing in the "full number of the Gentiles," a gleaning phase must follow the harvest to bring in still more! If the Jews had stepped forward to be God's harvesters, assumedly we Gentiles would be his gleaners. Because they disobeyed, we Gentiles who believe are privileged to be God's harvesters, which means the option to glean will be for whom? According to Old Testament Law, the privilege of gleaning must be reserved for people who were not involved in the harvest. The Jews! Will they want the privilege?

Ponder this for a scenario: When the 1 Thessalonians 4:17 Rapture happens, what effect will that momentous disappearance of millions of people have on all remaining earthlings—regardless of whether it turns out to be a pre-, a mid-, a post-tribulation event or something else?

Surely when the Rapture occurs, Muslims, Hindus, Buddhists, animists, atheists, skeptics and secularists will be totally flummoxed as people vanish, including some from unexpected contexts. Which group of people, then, will best be able to decode the mystery of history's far and away most enormous surprise?

The Jews!

If nothing else could ever compel Jewry to acknowledge Jesus as Messiah, surely the Rapture will be an eye-opener for them. Apparently Paul foresees that significant numbers of Jews will repent by acknowledging that the true Church has completed the mission originally given to them under divine oath.

As Jews plead for the opportunity to demonstrate genuine repentance, predictably the Lord will say, "Bless you at last! You are too late to engage in My harvest; it is finished. But I do require 144,000 of you to be my *gleaners*. Go forth across the earth and bring still more unbelievers to faith in Jesus of Nazareth, whom you now know was and is your Messiah. But know also that I give you a much more abbreviated span of time to accomplish what you must do for me."

Jeremiah is not alone in describing Old Testament Jewish believers as a firstfruits phase preceding an anticipated harvest out of the Gentile world. Paul himself echoes the Jeremiah 2:3 analogy in Romans 11:16:

> If the part of the dough offered as firstfruits is holy, then the whole batch is holy; if the root is holy, so are the branches.

Firstfruits harvest and gleaning are a *continuum* in Scripture. We are assured in Romans 11:25 that God's plan of the ages will not culminate with that continuum violated. If the 144,000 described in Revelation 7:1-8 are not the gleaners, I personally see nothing else in the New Testament that can be conceived of as completing the law via a post-harvest gleaning task force.

May Christians everywhere recognize the Great Commission as undeletable. Let's put it back into our Creeds, treasure it in our hearts and labor to facilitate its completion.

A NEW WAY TO REASON WITH SKEPTICS ABOUT GOD

Since who knows when, skeptics have been asking believers to "Define God!" Our customary reply, *God is a Spirit*, leads to their inevitable next demand that we "Define *Spirit*!" They smile bemusedly as we fumble for an answer.

The mere thought of actually being able to define—in precisely rational terms—the very nature of God strikes most Christians as bordering on sacrilege. The notion sounds brash, like attempting to cram infinity into a box. Being able to define God, even if possible, presumably would diminish our awe of him, and diminished awe might lead to diminished godliness. Just let everyone call him "God" and be satisfied!

Yet the underlying assumption that definition diminishes awe is wrong. Now that I know to define water as H_2O and understand what that means, I am even more impressed by water than when I, as a child, enjoyed splashing in it. How amazing that two invisible gases can become a liquid. Also, finding that oxygen linked with hydrogen supports life in even more ways than oxygen by itself is so intriguing. Definitions are usually hard to come by; yet once found, they lead to new discoveries and to increasingly greater degrees of awe.

The apostle Paul boldly averred in Romans 1:20:

Since the creation of the world God's invisible qualities—his eternal power and divine nature—have been *clearly seen* [not just "dimly sensed"], being understood from what has been made.

Paul seems to be assuring us that creation, correctly understood, attests to more than just God's existence. Apparently it actually points to the very nature of the Being we call God. How might that be true?

The Power of Corollaries to Connect

Logical skeptics understand the importance of corollaries. A corollary is a proposition that requires little or no proof due to its close association with one or more other propositions that are already proven. For example, a man who has never seen or heard of a lake or an ocean sees rain falling from the sky. He also sees rain forming rivulets that become streams and then rivers flowing away over the land. The factual evidence provided by experiencing land, sky, rain and rivers could enable that man to conclude that if enough rivers empty into the same lowland basin, they assuredly would form something that could be called "lake" on a small scale or even "ocean" on a larger scale.

He would be quite correct.

If creation teaches us to posit anything, it is this simple thesis: *Everything in the universe comes with at least one corollary!* Apparently God has been pleased to keep everything correlated at least in pairs if not in series. If so, however diligently we search, we will never find anything that is truly without a corollary!

Solid links with liquid and gas; land with sea and sky. Flora correlate with fauna; male with female; mammal with reptile; matter with energy. There are major and minor keys in music and primary and secondary colors in art. Touch correlates with our other senses, as does sweet with the other tastes. Consider how the four universal extents—length, width, height and time—correlate to comprise the enormous "continuum" that contains the entire cosmos, a mansion furnished with billions of galaxies. In popular parlance it is called the "space-time" continuum, but why hyphenate two words when a single synonym—extent—suffices?

Yet this is precisely where we get to test the above thesis. What, pray tell, may be "corollaried" with the extent continuum itself—that invisible but very real, absolutely indispensible entity wherein four dimensions, bonded together, provide both place and duration for matter and energy? Could there be another continuum formed by the bonding of an alternate set of dimensions? If so, that second continuum would serve to rescue the extent continuum from being without a corollary. To investigate this possibility, we begin by asking first, what is a dimension?

Our English word "dimension" comes from an identical Latin word, *dimension*, which means, guess what? Extent. The Latin root of "dimension" itself is *metiri*—"to measure." Thus, dimensions are things that enable various categories of measurement or comparison, such as longer versus shorter, wider versus narrower, higher versus lower, and newer versus older.

On that same basis, we all make measurements every day in ways that are distinct from the above four extent categories. Offered various ways to solve a problem, we apply *intellect* to measure degrees of logic. Offered options for entertainment, we get emotional about degrees of *pleasure*. Forced to face a harrowing experience, we summon a greater measure of *will* to endure. Are we not thus utilizing dimensions of an alternate category—*value* dimensions? Indeed we are!

Now, for a second step.

We credit our experience of length, width, height and time within our own bodies as due to those same four extent dimensions existing everywhere, right? So, let us also credit our experience of our three value dimensions—intellect, emotion and will—in our minds as due to those three value dimensions being just as much "everywhere" outside of us as the four extent dimensions are.

Third, as surely as those four extent dimensions form an extent continuum, let us credit our three value dimensions as comprising a just-as-much-everywhere *value* continuum. *Webster's New World Dictionary of the American Language* defines a continuum as "something whose parts cannot be separated nor even separately discerned."[1] That explains why it is impossible for something to have length, for example, but zero width or zero duration in time. All four extent dimensions inhere universally. They are inseparable; it is impossible for any one of them to exist alone.

Finally, let's posit our three invisible value dimensions as infinite and what do we have? Infinite intellect becomes *omniscience*. An infinite capacity for emotion is *omnisentience* (that new word I coined back in chapter 2). Infinite will becomes *omnipotence*. As surely as these three infinite values inhere just as inseparably to form an everywhere Value Continuum, who do we have? *God!*

Paul, then, quite correctly affirmed God's invisible qualities (values) along with His eternal power and divine nature as discernible, at least in terms of finding corollaries for what is testably true in our understanding of creation.

Indeed, it does make sense to postulate the extent continuum as a corollary to an invisible but equally real Value Continuum comprised of three just-as-real value dimensions! All scientists and skeptics everywhere acknowledge extent dimensions as basic to everything material. Posit God to them as an invisible, all-knowing, all-feeling, all-powerful Value Continuum who is also omnipresent in His corollary, the four-dimensional extent continuum they already know about. Now you have their attention!

Recently, I got about this far interacting with a French atheist by email. He replied, "This is the best approach to a concept of God that I have ever seen. But how does this approach lead to God being a Trinity?"

I replied, "As these three infinite value dimensions interface with each other in the Value Continuum, they become three different combinations of infinite intellect, emotion and will, i.e., three infinite Persons!

In one, ***intellect*** is primary with *emotion* and *will* shared, hence secondary.

In another, ***emotion*** is primary with *intellect* and *will* shared, hence secondary.

In a third, ***will*** is primary with *intellect* and *emotion* shared, hence secondary.

"Thus, we even know," I continued, "how each of these three invisible but all-powerful and omnipresent Persons distinguishes himself from his two fellow Beings. Each one knows which of the three infinite value dimensions is primary to him and which other two value dimensions he experiences by virtue of the eternal interfacing of the three value dimensions."

The atheist's response was, "I like this explanation!" I diagram it below.

The Triune Value Continuum
(I = Infinite Intellect, E = Infinite Emotion, W = Infinite Will)

First Person   Second Person   Third Person

These three Persons, co-existing as a single Value
Continuum, require God to be defined as
one Person who is three Persons.
In this quest to understand God, the Trinity is affirmed!

Imagine the above three diagrams merged as one to represent three infinite, invisible Persons coexisting as a *single* Value Continuum. God is thus one Person who is three Persons. In this quest to understand God, he is inherently triune! We begin to understand how John could designate Jesus as the "Word" who *is* God yet can also be described as One who is *with* God.

The above is a "brief" of just one of several original apologetic treatises from my self-published book *Unhidden*. Just as my first three books document "redemptive analogies" in human cultures, *Unhidden* is my quest to find a cosmos-wide redemptive analogy by uncovering corollaries linking theology with science.

For example, positing that God selected a single unifying motif to undergird the entire physical cosmos, I name a likely motif and then test it to see if it applies universally. Amazingly, it does.

I explore how God as the Value Continuum creates matter and energy replete with mass, charge, spin and conservation laws, not only *in*, but actually *of* and *from* the extent continuum itself.

I also explore the geology of our planet, seeking answers to crucial questions about the Genesis Flood, which, as you may know, is attested in hundreds of separate traditions worldwide.

Currently, used copies of *Unhidden* are being offered for sale online at exorbitant prices. The newest edition is available only on my website (www.donrichardsonbooksales.com) for not much more than the cost of the book you are reading now.

Contact me there.

ENDNOTES

Chapter 1: In the Crosshairs: *Love Wins* and *God Wins*

1. Rob Bell, *Love Wins* (New York: Harper Collins Publishers, 2011).
2. Thomas Newberry, *The Englishman's Greek New Testament* (Grand Rapids, MI: Zondervan Publishing House, 1970) first Zondervan printing; 11th printing 1982, p. 75. Newberry primarily used the Greek text of Stephens 1550, which he called the "common text" in England, from which he wrote in 1877. He offered further comments about the texts used in Section I of his Introduction, pp. v-x.
3. *New Strong's Concise Dictionary of the Words in the Greek New Testament* (Nashville, TN: Thomas Nelson Publishers, Inc., 1995), p. 3. In James Strong, *The New Strong's Exhaustive Concordance of the Bible* (Nashville, TN: Thomas Nelson, 1990).
4. Mark Galli, *God Wins: Heaven, Hell, and Why the Good News Is Better than* Love Wins (Carol Stream, IL: Tyndale House Publishers, 2011).
5. Ibid., p. 112.
6. Ibid., p. 109.
7. Ibid., p. 111.
8. Ibid.
9. Bell, *Love Wins*, p. 2.

Chapter 2: Why Did God "Leave a Door Ajar" for Evil?

1. C. S. Lewis, *Mere Christianity* (New York: The Macmillan Company, 1943; Macmillan Paperbacks edition 1970), p. 52.
2. C. S. Lewis, *The Screwtape Letters*, in *The Complete C. S. Lewis Signature Classics* (New York: HarperCollins, 2007; C. S. Lewis Pte. Ltd. edition 2002), p. 207.

Chapter 3: Does a Merely *Pyrrhic* Victory Over Evil Befit God?

1. Rob Bell, *Love Wins* (New York: Harper Collins Publishers, 2011), p. 2.
2. Mark Galli, *God Wins: Heaven, Hell, and Why the Good News Is Better than* Love Wins (Carol Stream, IL: Tyndale House Publishers, 2011), p. 126.
3. Ibid.
4. Bell, *Love Wins*, p. 4.

5. Ibid., p. 129.
6. Ibid.

Chapter 4: Is the Bible Really Vague About an "Age of Accountability"?

1. Irenaeus, "Against Heresies," III:16:4. In Ernest Cushing Richardson, James Donaldson and Arthur Cleveland Coxe, *The Ante-Nicene Fathers, Vol. 1: The Apostolic Fathers With Justin Martyr and Irenaeus* (New York: Cosimo, Inc., 2007), p. 442. The original publication date of *The Ante-Nicene Fathers, Volume 1—The Apostolic Fathers With Justin Martyr and Irenaeus* was 1885, with the first American printing in 1903 by Charles Scribner's Sons (New York).
2. Ibid., IV:28:3.
3. Matthew Henry, *Matthew Henry's Commentary on the Whole Bible* (Peabody, MA: Hendrickson Publishers, Inc., 1991), p. 2209.
4. Ibid.
5. Douglas J. Moo, *The NIV Application Commentary: Romans* (Grand Rapids, MI: Zondervan, 2000), p. 227.
6. Ibid.
7. F. F. Bruce, *Romans*, rev. ed.; in *Tyndale New Testament Commentaries*, Leon Morris, ed. (Grand Rapids, MI: Wm. B. Eerdmans Publishing Co., 1989), p. 149.
8. Ibid., p. 148.
9. Grant R. Osborne, *Romans*, in *The IVP New Testament Commentary Series*, Grant R. Osborne, general ed. (Downers Grove, IL: InterVarsity Press, 2004), p. 174.
10. Ibid., p. 177.
11. Ibid.
12. Both Harrison quotes in this section are from Frank E. Gaebelein, ed., *The Expositor's Bible Commentary*, vol. 10, *Romans-Galatians*, Everett F. Harrison, contributor on Romans (Grand Rapids, MI: Zondervan, 1976), p. 80.
13. R. Robert Mohler, Jr., "In the Shadow of Death—The Little Ones Are Safe with Jesus," June 5, 2005 online blog at http://www. albert mohler.com/2005/01/05/in-the-shadow-of-death-the-little-ones-are-safe-with-jesus/.
14. Ibid.
15. Ibid.
16. Ibid.
17. *New Strong's Concise Dictionary of the Words in the Hebrew Bible* (Nashville, TN: Thomas Nelson Publishers, Inc., 1995), p. 133. In James Strong, *The New Strong's Exhaustive Concordance of the Bible* (Nashville, TN: Thomas Nelson, 1990), p. 133, #7451.

Chapter 5: Measuring Infant Mortality

1. Wikipedia, "List of countries by Infant Mortality Rate." http://en.wikipedia.org/wiki/List_of_countries_by_infant_mortality_rate.

Figures are from http://en.wikipedia.org/wiki/List_of_countries_by_infant_mortality_rate#cite_note-2 United Nations World Population Prospects: 2011 revision, and from *CIA: The World Factbook–Infant Mortality Rate*, December 18, 2012.

2. Gina Kolata, "Study Finds 31% Rate of Miscarriage," *The New York Times* (July 1988). http://www.nytimes.com/1988/07/27/us/study-finds-31-rate-of-miscarriage.html.

3. Ibid.

4. "Pregnancy and Miscarriage," *WebMD: Infertility & Reproduction Health Center* (2012). http://www.webmd.com/infertility-and-reproduction/guide/pregnancy-miscarriage.

Chapter 8: General Revelation—Salvific for at Least a Few!

1. John Piper, *Let the Nations Be Glad! The Supremacy of God in Missions* (Grand Rapids, MI: Baker Academic, 1993, 2010), pp. 157-158.

Chapter 10: "Jobs" I Have Known or Know Of

1. Matthew Henry, *Matthew Henry's Commentary on the Whole Bible* (Peabody, MA: Hendrickson Publishers, Inc., 1991), p. 654.

2. Don Richardson, *Lords of the Earth* (Ventura, CA: Regal Books, 1977, 2nd ed. 2008), p. 169.

3. Don Richardson, *Peace Child* (Ventura, CA: Regal Books, 2005).

4. Don Richardson, *Eternity in Their Hearts* (Ventura, CA: Regal Books, 2005).

Chapter 11: Confronting "Name-ism"

1. John Piper, *Let the Nations Be Glad! The Supremacy of God in Missions* (Grand Rapids, MI: Baker Academic, 1993, 2010), p. 162.

2. Ibid., p. 171.

3. Ibid.

4. Ibid., pp. 157-158.

5. Ibid., p. 158.

6. Ibid.

7. Ibid., p. 162.

8. Ibid., p. 133.

9. Ibid.

10. Ibid., p. 137.

11. John Calvin, *The Acts of the Apostles*, 14-28, John W. Fraser, trans. (Grand Rapids, MI: Wm. B. Eerdmans Publishing Co., 1973), p 123.

12. Piper, *Let the Nations Be Glad! The Supremacy of God in Missions*, p. 154.

13. In 1792, Englishman William Carey published an 87-page booklet titled "An Enquiry into the Obligations of Christians, to Use Means for the Conversion of the Heathens. In which the Religious State of the Different Nations of the World, the Success of Former Undertakings, and the Practicability of Further Undertakings, Are Considered." (With such a long title, one almost didn't need to read the booklet!) In part because of the dissemination and readership of this publication,

a mission society was formed called Particular Baptist Society for the Propagation of the Gospel Amongst the Heathen.

Chapter 13: How Christianity Lost Its Innocence

1. Gordon R. Lewis, "Violence in the Name of Christ: The Significance of Augustine's Donatist Controversy for Today," *Journal of the Evangelical Theological Society*, 14:2 (June 1971), pp. 103-110. http://www.etsjets. org/files/JETS-PDFs/14/14-2/14-2-pp103-110_JETS.pdf.

2. Ibid., pp. 104, 109. Lewis's quotation of another author is cited as R. A. Knox, *Enthusiasm* (New York: Oxford University Press, 1959), p. 67.

3. "A Treatise Concerning the Correction of the Donatists or Epistle CLXXXV" (written by Augustine of Hippo in a letter to Boniface circa AD 417). In Philip Schaff, *Nicene and Post-Nicene Fathers Series 1, Volume 4—St. Augustine: The Writings Against the Manichæans and Against the Donatists* (Grand Rapids, MI: Wm. B. Eerdmans Publishing Co., 2009), pp. 112-115. http://www.tertullian.org/fathers2/NPNF1-04/npnf1-04-63.htm#P5899_2849983.

4. C. Gordon Olson, *Beyond Calvinism and Arminianism: An Inductive, Mediate Theology of Salvation* (Lynchburg, VA: Global Gospel Publishers, 1981, 3d ed. 2012), p. 447.

5. Ibid., p. 383. Quoting from Laurence M. Vance, *The Other Side of Calvinism*, 2d ed. (Pensacola, FL: Vance Publications, 1991), pp. 18-19.

6. Ibid., pp. 382-383.

7. Ibid., pp. 447-448. Citing Philip Schaff, *History of the Christian Church: Second Period—Ante-Nicene Christianity, A.D. 100-325, vol. II* (Grand Rapids, MI: Wm. B. Eerdmans Publishing Co., 1985), p. 502.

Chapter 14: So, Then, How *Does* God Manifest His Grace?

1. R. C. Sproul, *Willing to Believe* (Grand Rapids, MI: Baker Books, 1997).

2. Matthew Barrett, "Is Calvinism Anti-Missionary," Interview with Kenneth Stewart in *Credo*, 2:2 (March 2012), pp. 12-13. www.credomag. com/2012/04/16/is-calvinism-anti-missionary/.

3. Campus Crusade for Christ, "Have You Heard of the Four Spiritual Laws?" http://www.campuscrusade.com/fourlawseng.htm.

Chapter 15: How Christianity Lost Its Original Zeal

1. Rodney Stark, *Cities of God: The Real Story of How Christianity Became an Urban Movement and Conquered Rome* (San Francisco: HarperCollins Publishers, 2006), p. 67.

2. Thomas Cahill, *How the Irish Saved Civilization* (New York: Anchor Books, 1995).

3. Stark, *Cities of God*, p. 68.

4. From "Global Christianity: A Report on the Size and Distribution of the World's Christian Population," December 19, 2011. www.pewforum./ Christian/global-christianity-exec.aspx.

Chapter 16: Incomplete Creeds as Symptomatic Warnings

1. From The Holy Anaphora segment of "The Divine Liturgy of St. John Chrysostomos," http://www.preteristarchive.com/ChurchHistory/index.html.
2. "Mongol Empire," All About History, 2013. http://www.allabouthistory.org/mongol-empire.htm.
3. Eugene Myers Harrison, *Giants of the Missionary Trail* (Chicago: Scripture Press, 1954). http://www.wholesomewords.org/missions/giants/biocarey2.html.
4. Gustav Warneck, Campbell Macqueen Macleroy and George Robson, *Outline of a History of Protestant Missions from the Reformation to the Present Time: A Contribution to Modern Church History* (New York: Fleming H. Revell Co., 1901), p. 20.
5. Ibid.
6. Gregory Miller, "From Crusades to Homeland Defense," *Christian History and Biography*, no. 74 (April 2002). www.ctlibrary.com/ch/2002/issue74/9.31.html.

Appendix: A New Way to Reason with Skeptics About God

1. David B. Guralnik, ed., *Webster's New World Dictionary of the American Language*, 2nd college edition (New York: Simon & Schuster, 1982), p. 308.

SCRIPTURE INDEX

ACKNOWLEDGMENTS

My thanks to Bill Greig III, Stan Jantz and Gary Greig for their leadership of Regal Books, my publisher since the 1970s, and for encouraging me to write *Heaven Wins*.

Special thanks also to Carol, my wife, for her enthusiastic support in this project. Her expertise in grammar, syntax and logic has been immeasurably helpful to the task of reasoning carefully about very sensitive issues.

Also Available from Don Richardson

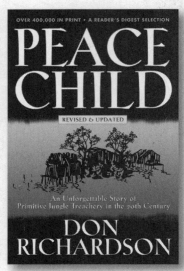
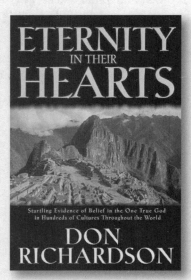
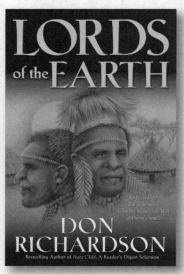